Hire Right. Keep Great People!

A 5-Stage Model to Build High-Performing Teams, Reduce Turnover, and Grow Future Leaders

Dr. Quendrida Whitmore

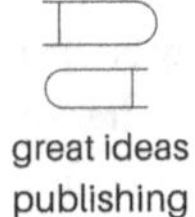

great ideas
publishing

Great Ideas Publishing

ISBN-13: 979-8-9937463-1-9 (print)
ISBN-13: 979-8-9937463-2-6 (ebook)
ISBN-13: 979-8-9937463-3-3 (audiobook)

Library of Congress Control Number: 2026938681

Published by Great Ideas Publishing
Bloomington, MN
greatideaspublishing.com

Contents

Introduction

When I decided to write my second book, after the first one on accountability, people asked how I decided what to write about next. Well, my publisher, being a research-based company, told me what I would do next. While we laugh, this is real talk.

The research shows that one of the top areas people struggle with is talent management.

According to global workforce research, roughly 70–75% of organizations report difficulty finding the skilled talent they need, making talent strategy one of the most significant opportunities and challenges facing modern organizations.

Many organizations struggle with talent shortages, retention, development, culture alignment, and keeping pace with the future of work.

Whether it's selecting the right people, developing a successful succession plan for upcoming openings, or developing talent to be ready for the next opportunity on time, people struggle with the people side of business.

I get it, it's not easy. There is no perfection in talent. It's art and science. I always say that if there were a formula for getting it right every time, someone would have bottled it already and made millions.

Common human resource (HR) conversations suggest that without structure, hiring outcomes can scatter evenly across high, average, and low performers.

That is, if we do nothing to ensure we remove bias, conduct in-depth interviews, and align on a clear need, we are at risk of repeatedly hiring mediocre-to-poor talent and trying to achieve great results with it.

The math ain't mathing!

This highlights the importance of deliberate selection over chance.

But selection is just part of the equation.

The Cost of Getting Talent Right or Wrong

In my career, I've made some exceptional hires and a few poor ones.

Looking back, almost every misstep traces back to a breakdown in the process: I rushed, skipped steps, didn't dig deep enough, or ignored red flags. Every bad hire taught me the same lesson: when you don't slow down and follow a structured, intentional process, you pay for it later.

Hiring right is hard.

But if we hire right, we then have the responsibility to develop that talent and give them access to information that supports their job performance and opportunities that allow them to grow and reach their potential. When I say grow, that could mean positionally, but it could also mean intellectually, collaboratively, and strategically. Growth that benefits them, the team, and the organization.

Talent is a continuous process and an intentional practice.

There is definitely a benefit to getting talent right. This could include results, culture, and even recruiting top talent.

On the other hand, there is also a cost to getting it wrong!

- Turnover

- Disengagement

- Disruption

- Dependency

- Stagnant Culture

When you get talent wrong, you often end up with a disengaged culture and lose great people. As widely noted in leadership circles, failing to hold poor performers accountable and effectively tolerating mediocrity are among the quickest ways to lose high-caliber talent who thrive in cultures of excellence.

Why?

What's that quote? "Iron sharpens iron." Top talent likes to be around other talented people.

Specifically, teams with clear performance norms retain top performers and discourage chronic underperformance.

Tolerance of poor performance damages morale and creates disruption.

When high performers consistently compensate for low performers, they experience burnout, disengagement, and disruption, a theme echoed in leadership commentary.

Disruption can take many forms

Disruption of results, disruption of ownership, or even disruption of communication and alignment.

Whatever form the disruption takes, it's devastating to the team and the results.

According to McKinsey & Company's article, *To Defend Against Disruption, Build A Thriving Workforce*, organizations must focus on hiring "thriving stars". These authors say thriving stars usually make up a small percentage of an organization but have an "outsized influence on organizations". Specifically, "thriving stars" are adaptable and resilient, approach work with flexibility and purpose, and earn their leaders' trust, allowing them to maintain high performance and influence those around them to do the same.

Thriving stars are a smaller percentage of many organizations (approximately 4%), but they have a mighty impact. With structure, intention, and focus, your talent process can cultivate, attract, and promote these thriving stars.

A Culture of Development Needs Intention

A few things to remember about talent management:

- Teams rarely fail from lack of talent; they fail from lack of intention.

- Great teams don't happen by accident.

- Talent is a daily practice, not a yearly event.

You must build repeatable, scalable routines to become great at talent. If you, as the leader, are not good at talent management, your team will never be great. Intention, focus, and routines make talent management a daily practice, not a yearly event.

To help build a daily practice, I developed a Talent Lifecycle Model that outlines the distinct steps of the talent process.

If you read my first book, you know I'm big on defining and aligning. So, before we dive into the Talent Lifecycle Model, let's align on what I mean by "high-performing teams" and "talent management".

High-performing Team: In *The Accountability Advantage* (the first book in the *Building a High-Performing Team* series), I called building a high-performing team the Avenger Effect, meaning it's the alignment of team, not individual goals, that saves the day. Specifically, a high-performing accountable team is "a group of talented individuals, each with unique powers, working toward a shared mission", achieving common goals rather than individual ones.

Talent management: The intentional, continuous process of attracting, selecting, developing, and advancing individuals in alignment with the organization's values, culture, and strategic goals, ensuring that the right people are in the right roles at the right time, doing work that matters.

It's not just about filling seats or hiring a team with a pulse.

It's about building capacity, creating belonging, and elevating performance, one high-potential, high-impact decision at a time, which is what I call *a **culture of development.***

An intentional *culture of development* isn't about launching new programs; it's a mindset and a leadership approach. It ensures talent is continuously grown, challenged, and supported. It means:

Structure: You have routines, systems, and expectations that guide how people are selected, onboarded, developed, and promoted. This includes clear talent review processes, Individual Development Plans (IDPs), feedback loops, and accountability mechanisms.

Intention: Leaders are not passive observers; they are active stewards of talent. They know the capabilities their teams need, are intentional about who gets opportunities, and are focused on helping individuals reach their next level of performance or potential.

Ownership: Everyone, from senior executives to frontline managers, owns a piece of the talent puzzle. This is not an HR job. Leaders understand they are responsible for developing people, providing visibility, creating stretch opportunities, and actively sponsoring future leaders.

When these three elements work together, you're no longer reacting to talent needs; you're shaping a pipeline through a culture of development, which is the ultimate goal of the Talent Lifecycle Model.

Coach Quen's Talent Lifecycle Model

As you dive into the lifecycle model, there are a few things I'd like to point out.

The steps take you from attraction to advancement in a clockwise pattern, but this model can start at any point.

Meaning, if you are filling a position, you would start with "attract" and work the model clockwise. However, if you're the leader of a functioning team, you may need to start at "belong" or "develop", then continue working the model clockwise.

Wherever your team is, that's where you start.

And if you do it well, you will be in a constant state of attraction to advancement, allowing you to build high-performing teams that deliver results.

Let's get into the model!

Coach Quen's Talent Lifecycle Model

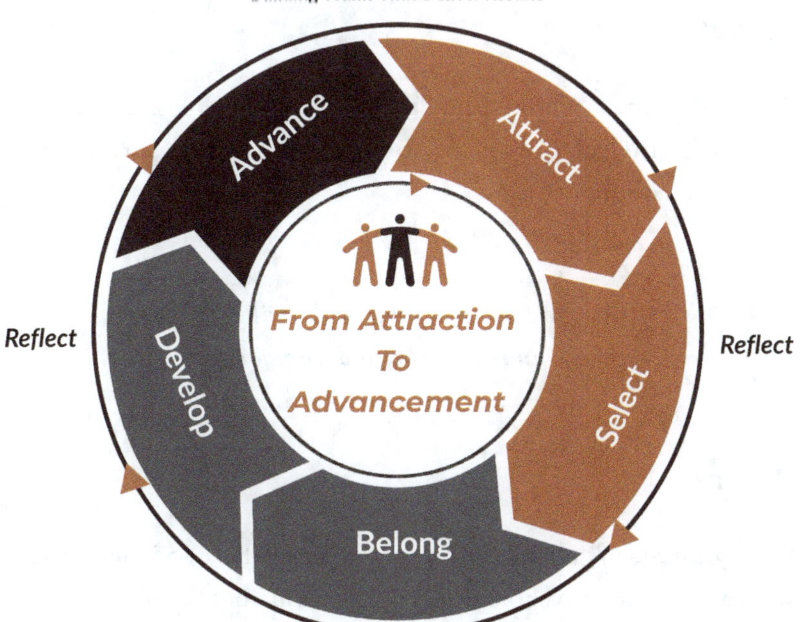

Attract

Attracting talent means intentionally showcasing your culture, values, and purpose to draw in individuals who align with your mission and are excited to contribute meaningfully.

> *When done well, attraction isn't about volume; it's about resonance. The right people see themselves in your vision and raise their hands to be part of it.*

Select

Selection is the structured, equitable process of choosing the right person for the role, based on alignment with both performance needs and cultural values.

> *It's not just who can do the job; it's who will thrive, elevate others, and help move the team forward.*

Belong

Belonging means creating an environment where individuals feel valued, seen, and psychologically safe to contribute their full selves.

> *Belonging is the bridge between hiring someone and unlocking their potential. It's how people move from "I work here" to "I matter here."*

Develop

Development is the continuous investment in a person's skills, confidence, and contribution, through coaching, feedback, stretch opportunities, and clarity of expectations.

Great leaders don't just manage performance; they grow people.

Advance

Advancing talent means recognizing, sponsoring, and promoting high-caliber individuals into expanded roles that match their readiness and potential.

Advancement isn't about favoritism or time served; it's about visibility, preparation, and building the future of your organization.

Reflect

Reflection is the continuous practice of assessing what's working, what's missing, and what must evolve across every stage of the talent lifecycle.

Reflection is how leaders stay intentional rather than reactive. It fuels smarter hiring, deeper development, and stronger succession.

You will notice, reflection is the circle around the entire model.

Reflection is not a one-time event; it's a continuous *leadership habit* that ensures decisions are aligned, inclusive, and performance-driven. Reflection should happen:

- **After hiring:** Did we get the right fit?

- **After onboarding:** Do they feel seen and supported?

- **After promotion:** Did we prepare them to succeed?

- **After exits:** What does this teach us about culture or leadership?

The Coach Quen Talent Lifecycle model will help you get on, stay on, and identify when you are off the track of talent management.

Plain Ol' Routines and Hard Work

Recently, an organization asked me, "What have you seen that is new and innovative in talent management?" I said talent management is about routines, not about being fancy. If you are looking for a new, innovative way to do talent, there are tons of AI tools out there to help you, but...

***NONE* will replace your daily talent routines.**

Artificial intelligence will absolutely enhance how we find talent, identify trends, deliver training, and anticipate future needs. There are some incredibly powerful tools available, and if you're resisting them, you're falling behind. It's time to get in the game.

But it's essential to understand: AI is *supplemental, not foundational.* These tools support your leadership; they don't replace it. Talent strategy still requires human judgment, relationship-building, and the courage to make the right call, not just the easy one. That part of the work will always be human.

Work It, Don't Just Read It

As in the first book in this series, this is a book to work with, not just read.

Get your pen, paper, notes, etc., and be ready to identify where you are fantastic and should share your knowledge with others, and where you need work, attention, and focus.

Remember, getting talent right is not about perfection.

It's about knowing when and where you need a tribe to help.

Remembering your biases, which may lead you down a path of confirmation rather than validation.

And building daily routines that help you get from attraction to advancement.

As the African proverb says, "it takes a village".

Talent is a community practice, not an individual match.

Sources

Chambers, E., Foulon, M., Handfield-Jones, H., Hankin, S., & Michaels, E. (1998). *The War for Talent*. McKinsey & Company.

Deloitte. (2023). *Global Human Capital Trends: New Fundamentals for a Boundaryless World*. Deloitte Insights.

ManpowerGroup. (2023). *Global Talent Shortage Survey: The New Human Age*. ManpowerGroup.

McKinsey & Company. (2024, May 8). *To defend against disruption, build a thriving workforce*. McKinsey & Company. https://rb.gy/eerstu

PwC. (2024). *PwC Global CEO Survey*. PricewaterhouseCoopers.

Smart, B. D. (2012). *Topgrading: The proven hiring and promoting method that turbocharges company performance* (3rd ed.). Portfolio/Penguin.

Society for Human Resource Management (SHRM). (2022). *Talent Acquisition Benchmarking Report*. SHRM.

Zentis, N. (2025, May 19). *Talent management challenges facing organizations today*. Institute of Organization Development. https://rb.gy/wlxxnj

PART I

ATTRACT
BUILDING A
TALENT MAGNET

Attract

Attracting talent is essential in the Talent Lifecycle.

When done well, attraction isn't about volume; it's about resonance. The right people see themselves in your vision and raise their hands to be part of it.

Attracting the right talent isn't just step one; it's the foundation on which every other part of the talent lifecycle is built. If you don't get this right, the rest of the cycle crumbles.

Think about it:

If the person you bring in lacks the skills or cultural alignment, your ability to develop, engage, or advance them is already compromised. You'll spend energy trying to "fix fit" instead of fueling growth. And fixing fit rarely works.

Key Takeaways:

- You can't coach your way out of a bad hire.

- You can't promote someone into potential they don't have.

- And you definitely can't build a high-performing team with mismatched talent.

That's why attraction must be intentional.

Let's dive into what it really takes to attract talent that not only qualifies on paper but thrives in your culture, aligns with your mission, and wants to grow with you.

Chapter One

Culture as a Recruiting Tool

Embrace the Truth About Your Culture

Does your organization actively use its culture as a recruiting tool? If not, you may be overlooking one of your most powerful advantages in attracting the right talent.

But before culture can attract, it must be *honest*.

That honesty starts with you.

What is your organizational culture, *really*? Not what's written on the wall. Not what you aspire to be someday. But what is actually modeled, rewarded, tolerated, and reinforced today?

Start by defining what your organization truly values, and be honest about it.

You cannot hire a change agent at the vice president (VP) level if your C-suite, led by your CEO, who values tradition above all, has no appetite for change. This doesn't create transformation; it creates chaos.

You've just set that VP up for resistance, frustration, and constant pushback. They believed what was said in the interview, that they were coming to be a change agent, even when their instincts picked up red flags along the way.

Don't rely on candidates to "call BS".
That's your responsibility as a leader.

Self-awareness matters. Be clear about what your culture *supports, embraces, and resists*, not what you hope it will become. If you genuinely want to change the culture, that work must start at the C-suite level. Any role below that does not have the authority to shift a culture set by top leadership.

Hiring change agents at the wrong level leads to:

- Frustration

- Misalignment

- Feelings of deception

And here's the truth:

A change agent will always be a change agent. With organizational support, they'll help you evolve. Without it, they'll challenge the status quo until they realize they can't win.

When that happens, they leave.

And when they leave, you're right back where you started, at **Attract**.

That's why honesty isn't just ethical.
It's strategic.

Once you embrace honesty, you can clearly identify what makes your culture attractive. Every organization has strengths, and some people will genuinely thrive in what you offer.

If your culture is rooted in history, tradition, and legacy, that's not a limitation; it's an advantage.

Some individuals value stability, continuity, and building on what already exists. On the other hand, some people thrive on change.

The key is knowing who fits your culture and speaking directly to them.

 Leadership Challenge: Cultural Attributes

Take the time to identify the *top five cultural attributes* that define your organization and would genuinely attract the right talent. Align all recruiters, interview panelists, and key decision-makers.

When you lead with what's true and compelling about your culture, you stop trying to appeal to everyone and start attracting the people who belong.

Clarify the mission, vision, and values to create alignment

Why Mission, Vision, & Values Matter.

They:

- Anchor Decision-Making

- Attract the Right Team

- Shape Culture and Drive Accountability

- Sustain Performance and Resilience

- Align Teams Across Silos

When leaders and teams are aligned on the *mission* (why we exist), the *vision* (where we're going), and the *values* (how we show up), decisions become clearer.

Top talent isn't just looking for a job; they're looking for *meaning*.

A clearly defined mission, vision, and values act like a magnet for candidates who resonate with your purpose and approach to work.

In seasons of change, growth, or challenge, these three elements become your foundation.

The Mission

Your mission is your why. It defines the purpose behind your work and the impact you are committed to delivering every day.

> **It's not just what you do, it's *why it matters*, to your team, your customers, and the world you serve.**

To attract the right talent, both you and the candidate must be aligned with the organization's mission. If either party is operating with its own separate agenda or is not fully bought into the mission, it's a setup for misalignment and eventual breakdown.

A lack of mission alignment doesn't just cause friction; it creates failure points across the entire talent lifecycle.

Hiring someone who isn't connected to the mission means you're not building for the long term. Shared purpose fuels shared success.

For example, Coach Quen's organizational mission is to "foster an environment of growth and innovation, where diverse talents are nurtured and turned into dynamic leadership capabilities, ensuring that every client can not only meet but exceed their personal and professional goals. We strive to create a more inclusive and equitable world, one leader at a time."

If I wanted to attract talent, I would look for people who believed in this mission. If you hire someone who is not aligned with the mission, you are hiring someone to do a job, not to grow with and for the business.

Doing a job is watching the clock, doing the steps, and running out the door when the day is done. Doing the job is not thriving. You want thriving talent. Thriving talent elevates itself and others.

Consider this: A scientist is building a team to research and develop solutions for climate change. But the candidates they hire don't believe in climate change.

No matter how skilled those individuals are, the team is *misaligned at its core.*
They don't share the mission.
They don't believe in the purpose.
They're not invested in the outcome.

Without alignment on the mission, there's no foundation for progress, only resistance, friction, and missed opportunities.

That's not just a hiring miss. It's a setup for failure.

A mission reminds people that their role, no matter how tactical, connects to a bigger purpose.

Without a clear mission, decisions become transactional. With it, they become intentional.

The Vision

Your vision paints a compelling picture of the future you're building and who you'll become along the way. It may not even be attainable, but it's inspirational.

> **It's not about being perfect; it's about being directional, aspirational, and bold enough to rally people forward.**

The vision keeps people in the game with you. There will always be tough times in every organization.

Difficult days.

But if the team you attract is bought into the vision, they will usually see themselves through the hard times, rally, and keep fighting for it.

Vision inspires teams to stretch. It gives them something to build toward.

In summary, you don't just hire someone who *can* do the job; you hire someone who *believes* in the work.

The Values

Your values are your how. They represent the behaviors, beliefs, and standards that shape how you lead, decide, and grow. Values set the behavioral standards. They clarify what's acceptable and what's not.

> **Values are not what's written on the wall; they're what shows up when things get hard. They're how culture becomes real.**

How you do something is just as important as what you do.

A values misalignment can quietly erode even the most well-intentioned teams.

Take this example: You hire someone who approaches work with a *win/lose mindset*, but your organization is rooted in collaboration and teamwork.

That's a mismatch.

Someone with a win/lose worldview believes that for them to win, someone else must lose. And while you may channel that competitiveness toward external goals, more often than not, that mindset turns inward, creating tension, turf wars, and siloed success.

Instead of building bridges across teams and departments, they stay in competition mode, missing critical opportunities to collaborate, share credit, and drive outcomes that benefit the *business, customer, and team.*

When values clash, progress slows, chips away at trust, and weakens culture from the inside out.

Values create *shared expectations* for how we collaborate, lead, and deliver.

Coach Quen Says: "Your mission tells people why you exist. Your vision shows them where you're headed. Your values tell them how to walk with you. Without these, even a great strategy will fail to scale."

Once you are clear on your culture, you can leverage it competitively in the attraction game.

Culture as a Competitive Advantage

In today's complex world, clarity of culture is no longer a "nice to have"; it's a *strategic advantage.*

High-performing talent is no longer just chasing paychecks; they're looking for purpose, belonging, and an organization that reflects who they are and what they value.

A paycheck may spark interest. But a mission fuels loyalty.

And a values-driven culture? That's what makes them stay.

When you're crystal clear about the kind of culture you offer, how your team works, leads, and supports one another, you don't just attract talent.

You attract *the right* talent.

People who are aligned with your values will *seek you out*, not just accept an offer.

If you're only selling compensation, you're competing on price. If you're selling culture, you're competing on purpose.

And purpose wins. Every time!

The Business Power of Inclusion

Inclusion fuels productivity, innovation, and revenue.

Research consistently shows that diverse leadership teams drive stronger business outcomes. For example, companies in the top quartile for ethnic diversity are approximately 36% more likely to outperform their peers financially, while those with strong gender diversity are about 25% more likely to achieve above-average profitability.

Why?

Because diversity drives better decision-making, deeper innovation, and stronger customer connections.

But what do we really mean when we talk about diversity and inclusion?

- **Diversity**: The collective mix of people across lived experiences, identities, perspectives, and ways of thinking that makes an organization stronger, more creative, and more resilient. This includes race, ethnicity, gender, age, education, background, neurodiversity, career experiences, and problem-solving approaches.

It's about who's in the room and the uniqueness each person brings.

- **Inclusion:** The intentional design of environments where every individual feels seen, heard, valued, and empowered to contribute fully. It's not just about having a seat at the table; it's about ensuring every voice matters. Inclusion fosters belonging, collaboration, psychological safety, and equity in opportunity and advancement.

When diversity is invited, and inclusion is embedded, organizations unlock the full potential of their people, sparking innovation, building trust, and growing leaders at every level.

> **A culture of inclusion doesn't just retain talent, it attracts it.**

Being known for your inclusive culture becomes a competitive edge. It enhances your reputation, strengthens your employer brand, and makes your organization one that top talent seeks rather than avoids.

Change Your Tactics

For organizations struggling to find top talent, if you are asking, *"Where do I find the best talent?"* My response?

Stop fishing in the same pond.

If you want a more diverse, innovative, and high-performing work-force, you must expand your network and diversify the talent pools you recruit from.

Yes, it's true, talent knows talent. Your current team can be a great source of referrals. But keep in mind that referred candidates often resemble the people who refer them. As the saying goes, *birds of a feather flock together.*

To build a team that reflects the world around you and the customers you serve, you must intentionally vary your tactics.

- ***Look in new places:*** Attend different career fairs, build partnerships with diverse organizations, and connect with talent in adjacent industries.

- ***Ask different questions:*** To broaden your definition of what great talent looks like.

- ***Use different tools:*** Go beyond your usual platforms and networks.

There's a common leadership saying: If you only look where you've always looked, you'll keep finding what you've always found. Inclusion isn't just a value; it's a recruitment strategy.

Now, let's dive into clearly defining the role and the talent needed for the future of the organization.

Sources

Chatman, J. A. (1991). Matching people and organizations: Selection and socialization in public accounting firms. *Academy of Management Journal, 34*(3), 459–484. https://doi.org/10.2307/256404

Deloitte. (2018). *The diversity and inclusion revolution: Eight powerful truths.* Deloitte Insights. https://rb.gy/yocdzy

Gallup. (2023). *State of the global workplace 2023 report: The voice of the world's employees.* Gallup. https://rb.gy/s8ukxk

Hunt, V., Layton, D., & Prince, S. (2015). *Why diversity matters.* McKinsey & Company. https://rb.gy/6smz3w

Hunt, V., Prince, S., Dixon-Fyle, S., & Yee, L. (2020). *Diversity wins: How inclusion matters.* McKinsey & Company. https://rb.gy/igoux3

Kotter, J. P., & Heskett, J. L. (1992). *Corporate culture and performance.* Free Press.

McPherson, M., Smith-Lovin, L., & Cook, J. M. (2001). Birds of a feather: Homophily in social networks. *Annual Review of Sociology, 27,* 415–444. https://doi.org/10.1146/annurev.soc.27.1.415

Chapter Two

Define the Role, Define the Future

When it comes to building a high-performing team, defining the role is the first leadership decision that shapes your future. The choices you make at this stage don't just influence who applies; they determine whether the person you hire can help you win now and evolve tomorrow.

Look Forward, Not Back

The most common mistake leaders make is hiring for the organization they *have* rather than the one they *are evolving into*. That's a recipe for stagnation. Continuing to replace what you have is the easy button, and could create:

- Status quo

- Missed opportunity to solve a persistent business gap

- Missed opportunity to evolve and innovate

- Lack of development for the total team

- Organizational stagnation

Before you post a job, pause and evaluate your organizational structure. If you just said, I don't have time for that, consider two things:

- Time is a precious commodity, and you will cost yourself more time and resources hiring the wrong person or hiring the wrong position

- How can you build this reflection into your hiring routine to ensure there is enough time in the plan to evaluate the structure?

Remember, it's the daily practices that make an excellent talent manager.

You must answer the following questions:

- Where is your team today?

- Where are you going in the next 1, 3, or 5 years?

- What will success look like in that future state, and what kind of role needs to exist to get you there?

Creating a 1, 3, or 5-year plan doesn't mean locking yourself into a rigid roadmap. In today's fast-moving business environment, agility is essential. This kind of planning simply means you've taken the time to clarify the direction you want to move in, and you've outlined a thoughtful path to help you get there. It's not about predicting every step, but about being intentional with your goals and prepared to pivot as needed.

Organizational Flow Chart

Coach Quen's Tip: When creating an organizational flow chart, start with structure, not people.

Begin by identifying the core roles and responsibilities the organization needs to succeed and grow. Ask yourself:

> ***What roles are critical for where we're going, not just where we are?***

Resist the urge to plug names into boxes too early. Design the chart around what the business needs, not around who's currently on the team.

Once the structure is clear, go back and assess where your current talent fits. Match people to roles based on their skills, capacity, and potential, not tenure or likability.

If you're struggling to place someone in a role confidently, that's an indicator:

- Leadership may be needed to **develop their gaps**, or

- A different decision may be required about their future fit.

Structure first. Talent second. Strategy always.

📖 Storytime: Structure is the Foundation

I once worked with an organization that needed to downsize during a challenging business period. Parts of the company had been sold, and leadership needed clarity on which roles were still essential and who should be responsible for them.

We started with the organizational chart, but with **no names in the boxes.**

First, we defined each role by its core responsibilities and aligned those responsibilities to the organization's mission. Our guiding questions were simple: *What are the core responsibilities of this position, and why is it essential for the organization today and in the future?*

Only after we had a clear organizational structure with the right roles in place did we begin evaluating talent against those positions.

Too often, organizations do this in reverse, trying to design the structure around the people they currently have. When you build the organization that way, you risk staying anchored to the past instead of evolving toward what the business actually needs next.

Structure must come first. Once the structure is clear, the talent decisions become much easier to make.

Field Leadership: Align Structure to Strategy, Not Preference

If you lead in the field, start by asking a simple but powerful question:

> **Does the current alignment still serve the business?**

What the business needs to be successful should always drive your structure, not individual preferences.

That said, *short-term support is different from long-term misalignment.* For example, if you reduce a leader's span, say, fewer locations for the first 90 days, to help them get acclimated, that's strategic support. It's a temporary investment to get them up and running.

But if the only way an individual can succeed is by permanently changing the business structure around them, it's time to pause and ask tough questions.

Why? Because:

- They may not yet have the skills or capacity.

- You may not have provided the development or coaching they needed.

- Or, it may simply be a bad fit for the role.

If you have to change the business *to make someone successful,* you may not have the right person for the job.

Great leaders balance support with accountability. Don't confuse adjusting for growth with lowering the bar.

In summary...

Don't hire for yesterday's job.
Hire for today's gaps and tomorrow's growth.

The Role Behind the Role

Job descriptions (JD) are often bloated or vague. They need to be that way, as they are often used to ensure the organization is legally protected. But great hiring starts with positional clarity, not just what the job description *says*, but what the JD *means*. Remember, the job isn't just about "what"; it's about the "how" and why the position matters to the organization.

Ask yourself:

- What are the core responsibilities of this role that drive the business forward?

- What are the key decisions this role should own?

- What does success look like in six months? In 12 months?

Think of it as narrowing the scope: You're defining not just the tasks, but the impact this role should make.

Clarity reduces misalignment. And misalignment drains momentum.

 **Leadership Challenge: Define the 1-2-3**

Here's a simple tool I use with clients when defining a role:

> **What are the 1, 2, or 3 most important outcomes this role must deliver to be successful?**

Not a list of 20 tasks. Not everything the last person did. Just the big levers that matter most.

Once you've defined those 1-2-3 outcomes:

- Use them to build **targeted interview questions**

- Align your **performance goals**

- Ensure the recruiter, interviewers, the hiring manager, and the candidate are **on the same page**

Clarity in the beginning protects performance in the end.

Bottom Line: Define to Align

Defining the role isn't a formality. It's a strategic act. When you define with intention, you set the stage to attract aligned, capable, and purpose-driven talent.

If you skip this step, or phone it in, you'll end up solving the *wrong problem with the wrong person.*

And when that happens, the cost isn't just turnover. It's lost time, team disruption, missed momentum, and results.

Define the role well, and you define your future well.

Don't Go to the Grocery Store Hungry

I said it in my first book, and I'll say it again: never go to the grocery store hungry.

Why? Because when you walk in without a plan, you come out with snacks, like chocolate, chips, and soda, not foods that help you thrive.

The same is true for hiring.

When you leave critical roles unplanned or wait until it's urgent, you fall into reactive hiring: relying on who's available, who you like, or who feels familiar.

That's when you make short-term choices that hurt long-term performance.

You must have a clear definition of the role and a plan to attract the right candidates.

Having a role definition is your hiring meal plan or grocery list. It gives you clarity on what the business needs to grow, and a filter for evaluating if a candidate can deliver.

Be Involved in Your Recruitment Process

Through it all, you must stay involved in the attraction process.

Some hiring leaders assume that recruitment is solely the recruiter's responsibility, hard stop. While recruiters may *own the* process, if the attraction phase is broken, *you're the one who pays the price.*

You must stay actively engaged throughout the recruitment journey. This means:

- Understanding the recruitment process,

- Aligning with your recruiters on the role, culture, and competencies needed, and

- Realigning quickly when the candidate flow isn't meeting expectations.

Once I learned the importance of being involved in the hiring process, I always started with a recruiter kick-off meeting. We aligned on the role, team dynamics, culture fit, and key behaviors. If the recruiter was sending great candidates, I let them know. If they weren't, we adjusted, meeting weekly to discuss where the candidates were falling short and why.

Some leaders might say, "I don't have time for that."

I agree! Time is always challenging, but investing time here can prevent much larger problems down the road.

Dragging out an open role, or worse, hiring the "best of the worst", creates ripple effects:

- Poor performance and unmet goals,

- Disruption to team dynamics,

- Burnout for the team covering the gap.

But when you and a strong recruiter are aligned? *Magic happens.* You attract the right people, move faster, and set new hires up for success.

Be involved and aligned. Together, you and your recruiter can gain or lose your top talent.

After you have attracted the right talent, you need an intentional selection process to get the best!

Sources

Breaugh, J. A. (2013). Employee recruitment. *Annual Review of Psychology, 64*, 389–416. https://doi.org/10.1146/annurev-psych-113011-143757

Cable, D. M., & Turban, D. B. (2001). Establishing the dimensions, sources, and value of job seekers' employer knowledge during recruitment. *Research in Personnel and Human Resources Management, 20*, 115–163.

Campion, M. A., Mumford, T. V., Morgeson, F. P., & Nahrgang, J. D. (2005). Work redesign: Eight obstacles and opportunities. *Human Resource Management, 44*(4), 367–390. https://doi.org/10.1002/hrm.20080

Cappelli, P. (2008). *Talent on demand: Managing talent in an age of uncertainty.* Harvard Business School Press.

Collins, C. J., & Stevens, C. K. (2002). The relationship between early recruitment-related activities and the application decisions of new labor-market entrants. *Journal of Applied Psychology, 87*(6), 1121–1133. https://doi.org/10.1037/0021-9010.87.6.1121

Morgeson, F. P., & Campion, M. A. (2000). Work design. In N. Chmiel (Ed.), *Introduction to work and organizational psychology: A European perspective* (pp. 423–452). Blackwell.

Rothwell, W. J. (2010). *Effective succession planning: Ensuring leadership continuity and building talent from within* (4th ed.). AMACOM.

PART II

SELECT
STRUCTURE
OVER
SUBJECTIVITY

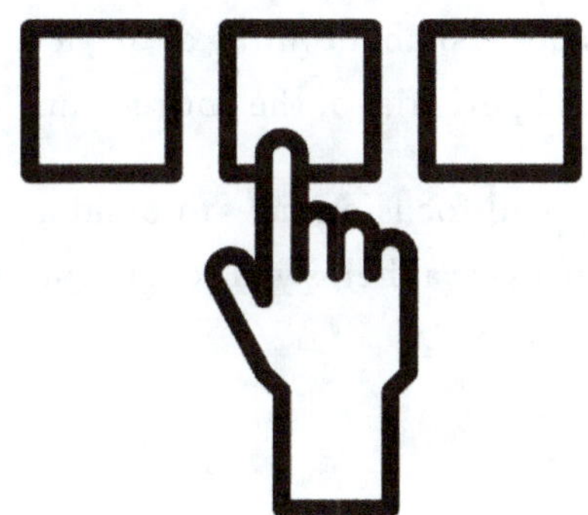

Select

Selecting the right talent is one of the most important decisions a leader makes. The people you bring onto your team shape the culture, influence performance, and determine how effectively the organization executes its strategy.

When the right person is selected, results accelerate and momentum builds.

When the wrong person is hired, leaders often spend months or even years trying to manage around the gap.

Talent selection is not just about filling a role; it is about protecting the performance and potential of the entire team.

In this section, we will focus on how to build a structured, intentional selection process that helps you consistently identify and hire great talent.

Chapter Three

The Power of a Structured Selection Process

You've done the work, clarified the role, aligned the mission, vision, and values, and broadened your reach to attract diverse, high-potential candidates. (Shout-out to Part I!) Now, it's time to protect that investment with a structured, intentional selection process.

This section will walk you through building a structure to help you select not just a qualified candidate, but the *right* one.

Achieve Alignment

Your role as the hiring leader is to achieve alignment.

Aligning simply means achieving "a position of agreement or alliance".

A critical part of this is aligning with your interview panel. Anyone supporting the hiring process needs to understand three things:

1. The goal of the hire.

2. Their role in the process.

3. What success looks like at the end of selection.

The essential point:

The interview panel doesn't get to ask whatever questions they *want*; they must ask the questions you *need to* uncover the truth about fit, skill, and potential.

📖 Storytime: My Favorite Question

I once led the selection process for a leadership role. During the kickoff meeting, a few panelists began sharing their "favorite" interview questions. Not one of them aligned with the competencies or priorities we had defined for the role. That moment made something clear: everyone thinks they're a great interviewer. Some are, some are not. One even said, "My favorite question to ask is: if you were a layer of a Big Mac, what layer would you be and why?"

What? What does that tell you?

I quickly began to realign and clarify.

Lesson Learned: I realized then the need to always align with the interview panel. No matter the experience level. A quick alignment meeting ensures everyone is on the same page.

That's where you, as the hiring leader, must take control.

- Clarify the non-negotiables. What does this person need to do, lead, or influence?

- Craft interview questions with purpose. Build them to reveal behaviors, thinking patterns, and cultural fit (hopefully, your organization has interview guides you can leverage).

- Ensure consistency across panelists. Assign focus areas so the same questions aren't repeated, and so nothing critical gets missed.

Structured interviews yield better hires. Random interviews yield random results.

Team and Behavioral Fit

Now that you've aligned on culture and clarified the role's core responsibilities, it's time to focus on team *and behavioral fit.*

So what do I mean by that? We lightly introduced the concept in the values section.

Someone may get the job done, but not do it the right way. In other words, they may deliver results, but in ways that undermine your organization's values, culture, or team dynamics.

Your interview panel must be aligned not just on performance expectations, but also on the specific behaviors that define success in your organization. For example, are you looking for someone who is:

- Collaborative in their approach?

- Resourceful when faced with ambiguity?

- Data-driven in decision-making?

- Curious when navigating challenges?

These aren't just soft skills; they are critical success behaviors. And if your interviewers aren't clear on them, they won't ask the right questions to uncover them.

Behavioral misalignment doesn't just disrupt performance; it breaks trust and team cohesion.

As the hiring leader, you must guide the panel to probe for these core behaviors during interviews. Because when you hire someone who reflects both the values and ways of working your team embodies, you're not just filling a seat, you're strengthening the culture

Reducing Bias

Many leaders are quick to point out bias in others, yet do little to examine their own. Here's the truth: *we all have biases.* The goal isn't to pretend biases don't exist; the goal is to recognize them and actively work to reduce their impact.

In interviews, bias often shows up as *liking someone*. An instant connection can feel powerful:

"We grew up the same way."

"We think alike."

"They remind me of me."

That doesn't mean you've found the right hire. It simply means you've found someone you might enjoy having dinner with, or maybe even a new best friend.

> **Chemistry is not competence.**

In all seriousness, bias shows up in *every* interview. You can't eliminate it entirely, but you *can* identify it, slow it down, and reduce its influence. This is where a structured interview process becomes critical. It creates consistency, discipline, and guardrails against snap judgments.

Before interviews even begin, leaders and interview panels must understand the most commonly known biases that show up in selection decisions:

- **Rater Bias:** Rater bias occurs when an interviewer consistently rates candidates higher or lower based on personal standards, preferences, or leniency, rather than objective criteria tied to the role.

- **Halo/Horns Effect:** The halo effect occurs when a single positive trait (such as confidence or charisma) leads an interviewer to assume the candidate is strong across all areas.

The horns effect is the opposite; one perceived weakness overshadows everything else. These are usually based on the interviewer's preferences or values.

- **Confirmation Bias:** Confirmation bias occurs when interviewers form an early opinion about a candidate and then ask questions or interpret answers in ways that confirm that belief, rather than objectively assessing the candidate's fit and capabilities.

Let me give you an example. I love resilient people. If they have failed and bounced back, I usually find chemistry with them. Well, someone who is resilient may be the right person, but if I keep asking questions about this competency, I will get what I want, not necessarily the truth about the candidate's total qualifications.

Additionally, I tend to get irritated easily when people lack self-awareness or self-accountability. Someone could have been the best interviewee ever, but if I don't think they are self-aware, I don't like them. They literally could have put the first man on the moon or discovered electricity. I don't care!

While these are funny but true examples, if I did nothing to address my bias, I could really land in a bad place: hiring the exact wrong person, addressing poor performance, and then starting from the very beginning of attracting again.

> **Bias doesn't disappear when ignored. It grows when unchecked.**

By naming these biases upfront and committing to a structured process, leaders significantly improve the quality, fairness, and effectiveness of their hiring decisions.

Process Beats Preference Every Time

Here's the truth: discipline and routines, not fancy events, build great talent pipelines.

📖 Storytime: Routines Matter

One organization I'm familiar with did many things right with talent. They used structured interviews, focused on competency-based leadership, and invested heavily in development. But one strategy, despite all the effort and resources, missed the mark.

Each year, they poured time, money, and energy into a high-profile conference. Their goal was to recruit top-tier talent, but their approach was to throw *the party of the year*. The event became legendary. People fought to get on the guest list. It had all the glitter, glam, and buzz.

But when you stepped back and looked at the data?

It didn't deliver.

Yes, a few hires came out of it, but many struggled to succeed in the culture. The turnover was high. The internal narrative shifted: *"What's going on over there? Why can't talented hires thrive?"*

Unfair or not, perception became reality.

> **Lesson Learned:** It's not just about *attracting talent*. It's about attracting the *right* talent and ensuring your culture is ready to support and keep them. That requires honesty, structure, and alignment.

As I discussed in the *Attract* chapters:
You have to be truthful about your culture, not what's written on the walls, but what truly exists within your organization.

Because if the culture doesn't match the promise, top talent will leave, and you'll be right back at the beginning of the cycle.

Flashy events may spark interest, but structure sustains success.

The Candidate Experience Matters

It never ceases to amaze me how often I hear the same story from candidates:

"The recruiter was enthusiastic. I sent my resume, shared my availability to speak with the next level, and then... nothing."

There are few good reasons to ghost a candidate.

Whether the role was put on hold, filled by another applicant, or no longer needed, there are a hundred reasons why a candidate doesn't move forward. But none of those reasons justify silence.

Your Candidate Experience = Your Reputation

Think of each candidate as a customer. A dissatisfied customer doesn't just walk away; they tell others.

Research on customer experience shows that dissatisfied customers often share negative experiences widely, telling an average of 9–15 people about a poor experience.

The same is true for job candidates.

Your hiring process sends a message. It speaks to your values, your professionalism, and your respect for people. Treat every candidate with intentionality, clarity, and respect, even when the answer is no.

The Culture of the Interview

The culture you create during an interview is critical to the candidate's experience and to the quality of information you gather.

Some interviewers swing too far in one direction:

- They *love* everyone, making candidates feel like they've found a new best friend.

- Or they do the opposite, trying to put candidates on edge to "see how they react".

Intimidation is not insight.

If you put someone into a stress mindset, you'll get a stress response. That's not how most people show up at work every day. Don't test people. Don't try to trip them up. And don't confuse pressure for performance.

Your role as an interviewer is to create an environment that is *comfortable enough to get the real person, but formal enough to signal that this is a serious, intentional process.*

That balance is where the truth shows up.

It's the only way you can genuinely assess:

- Cultural alignment

- Communication style

- Judgment and decision-making

- Real experiences, not rehearsed or fear-based responses

Your goal is to assess the person, not their anxiety.

When you get the interview culture right, you don't just learn if someone *can* do the job. You learn how they'll actually show up once they're on the team.

Be Transparent and Thoughtful

If someone isn't moving forward, communicate that. While you may not owe external candidates detailed feedback, offer as much clarity as possible. Close the loop.

With *internal candidates*, transparency is not optional; it's a responsibility. If you invited them to interview, you owe them meaningful feedback. Otherwise, you risk disengagement, resentment, and even attrition.

I've coached many professionals who were fully invested in their companies... until they were passed over for a promotion without *explanation.* They felt manipulated, ignored, and gaslit.

And when people feel that way, *they leave.*

Now that I've mentioned interviewing multiple times, let's get into it.

Sources

Campion, M. A., Palmer, D. K., & Campion, J. E. (1997). A review of structure in the selection interview. *Personnel Psychology, 50*(3), 655–702.

Chapman, D. S., Uggerslev, K. L., Carroll, S. A., Piasentin, K. A., & Jones, D. A. (2005). Applicant attraction to organizations and job choice: A meta-analytic review of the correlates of recruiting outcomes. *Journal of Applied Psychology, 90*(5), 928–944. https://doi.org/10.1037/0021-9010.90.5.928

Hausknecht, J. P., Day, D. V., & Thomas, S. C. (2004). Applicant reactions to selection procedures: An updated model and meta-analysis. *Personnel Psychology, 57*(3), 639–683. https://doi.org/10.1111/j.1744-6570.2004.00003.x

Levashina, J., Hartwell, C. J., Morgeson, F. P., & Campion, M. A. (2014). The structured employment interview: Narrative and quantitative review of the research literature. *Personnel Psychology, 67*(1), 241–293. https://doi.org/10.1111/peps.12052

Oxford University Press. (2026). *Aligning Definition.* Google.com. https://rb.gy/zwytcg

Richins, M. L. (1983). Negative word-of-mouth by dissatisfied consumers: A pilot study. *Journal of Marketing, 47*(1), 68–78. https://doi.org/10.1177/002224298304700107

Schmidt, F. L., & Hunter, J. E. (1998). The validity and utility of selection methods in personnel psychology: Practical and theoretical implications of 85 years of research findings. *Psychological Bulletin, 124*(2), 262–274. https://doi.org/10.1037/0033-2909.124.2.262

White House Office of Consumer Affairs. (2014). *Customer experience impact report.*

Chapter Four

Interviewing That Works

There are a few things that make interviews more effective.

- Competency-based interviewing

- Pre-work

- Structured Questions

- Interview Probes

Let's start with competencies.

Shared Language: The Power of Competencies

Competencies provide a common language, a foundational tool for aligning, defining, and assessing talent across your organization.

Yet, many organizations overlook them. In the long list of priorities, developing a clear competency framework often falls toward the bottom. But here's the truth:

Competencies shouldn't be an afterthought; they should be at the top of the list.

Without shared competencies, each leader is left to define what "good" looks like for themselves. That creates confusion, misalignment, and inconsistency, not because of poor intent, but because of a lack of clarity.

When used effectively, competencies:

- Provide a standardized way to evaluate talent, performance, and potential.

- Help teams speak the same language and share the same definitions for behaviors such as communication, collaboration, and driving results.

- Ensure your interview panels and leaders are aligned, not just on the words, but on what those words look like in action.

Example: If five people are interviewing a candidate and all value "collaboration", but define it differently, you're not assessing the same thing.

A competency framework ensures that, across your organization, you assess, develop, and promote talent based on aligned, intentional, and strategic behaviors rather than individual preferences.

Interview Types: Behavioral and Motivational

To accurately assess a candidate, start by choosing the right type of interview.

Many leaders lean on hypothetical questions, asking candidates what they would do in a given scenario. The problem? Most people are smart enough to know not to say they'd handle it poorly.

For example, if you ask, "What would you do if a customer started yelling at you?", you're unlikely to hear, "I'd yell back or punch them."

While that's an extreme example, it highlights the flaw in hypothetical scenarios: they often invite idealized, not realistic, responses.

Instead, focus on what candidates have actually done. This gives you a better prediction of how they'll perform in the future.

Two powerful types of interview questions help assess behavior and fit: Behavioral and Motivational.

Behavioral Interview Questions

Behavioral interviews focus on how a candidate has acted in specific, real-life situations. The underlying belief is: past behavior is the best predictor of future performance.

Typical format:

"Tell me about a time when you had to deal with a difficult teammate. What did you do?"

What it reveals:

- Actual experiences

- Core competencies like collaboration, accountability, or conflict resolution

- Evidence of skills in action

Common framework:

Structured behavioral interview techniques often use frameworks such as the STAR method to help candidates describe specific situations, actions, and outcomes, allowing interviewers to assess real behavior rather than hypothetical responses.

STAR – Situation, Task, Action, Result

Motivational Interview Questions

Motivational questions uncover what drives a candidate, their purpose, values, and alignment with your organization's culture and mission. They explore why someone wants the role and what fuels their performance.

Typical questions include:

"What part of your current job energizes you the most?"
"Why are you interested in this role at this point in your career?"
"What kind of environment brings out your best work?"

Bonus tactic:

Motivation can also be explored within behavioral questions. After hearing the candidate's response, ask:

"Why was that important to you?"

This helps you uncover deeper motivations and value alignment.

Why it matters: Fit isn't just about skill; it's about drive, purpose, and values alignment. When someone is motivated by the same things your organization stands for, performance and engagement follow.

Probe Questions in Interviewing

Probe questions are among the most underutilized tools in interviews. I will spend some time here because they are that important, and many leaders do not probe during interviews.

Which is a BIG mistake.

Probe questions are follow-up questions used during an interview to dig deeper into a candidate's initial response. They're designed to clarify, expand on, or challenge the answer to gain a fuller understanding of the candidate's actual behavior, thinking process, and experience.

Probe questions often begin with phrases like:

- *"Can you tell me more about that?"*

- *"What specifically did you do?"*

- *"How did that decision impact the team?"*

- *"What was the result?"*

- *"Why did you approach it that way?"* (Yay, a motivational probe)

Probe questions are vitally important for a few reasons:

1. Reveal Depth, Not Just Surface

Initial answers often skim the surface or use vague language. Probing helps peel back the layers and uncover:

- Specific behaviors and actions

- Decision-making rationale

- Emotional intelligence and interpersonal dynamics

2. Clarify Ambiguities

Candidates may generalize or make assumptions in their responses. Probing helps clarify:

- Who did what

- What the situation actually involved

- The candidate's true role and contribution

3. Distinguish Real Experience from Theory

Without probes, candidates may give hypothetical or rehearsed responses. Probing shifts the focus from "what sounds good" to "what actually happened".

Example:

Q: "Tell me about a time you led a project."

A: "We worked hard and got it done on time."

Probe: *"What was your specific role on the team? What challenges did you personally face, and how did you overcome them?"*

4. Reduce Bias and Increase Accuracy

When all interviewers use probes consistently, it reduces over-reliance on first impressions or "gut feelings" and supports a structured, evidence-based evaluation process.

5. Assess Self-Awareness and Reflection

How someone responds to a probe often reveals whether they've truly reflected on their experiences. Strong candidates can explain not just what they did, but why it mattered and what they learned.

📖 Storytime: The Power of the Probe

I once interviewed a leader. Early in the conversation, I noticed the candidate stayed at a very high level and breezed over details. That's a signal, so I started probing.

At one point, I asked him about a specific process he said he had fixed in his building: I asked:

- *What was broken?*

- *How did it become broken?*

- *What was actually happening day to day?*

- *And most importantly, what did you do to fix it?*

I asked these questions in several ways, trying to understand the root of the issue. With each probe, he became more irritated and clearly wanted me to move on.

I didn't.

Finally, frustrated, he said:

"I had a bunch of women in the process, and they messed up everything because they couldn't do the work."

Oh. Wow.

That was exactly what I needed to hear. Needless to say, he was not hired.

Here's the lesson: *if I had accepted his first, second, or even third answer, I might have offered him the job. The probe revealed what surface-level answers never would: his mindset, his biases, and how he truly led people.*

Lesson Learned: Probe questions aren't for the candidate's comfort. They're for your understanding.

And when used well, they protect your culture, your team, and your results.

Self-Awareness: A Leadership Essential

Self-awareness is one of the most valuable traits to assess during interviews. A strong candidate will not only understand their strengths but also be candid about their areas for growth, which I often call development opportunities. A lack of self-awareness isn't just a red flag; it can be a warning sign of poor leadership maturity or unchecked ego.

Let's break it down:

Strengths

A self-aware candidate can clearly articulate what they're great at. This shows they understand the unique value they bring to your organization or to the role and how they plan to make an impact.

If someone can't articulate their strengths, they may struggle to find their place or contribute meaningfully to the team.

I once asked a candidate to describe their strengths, and their response was, *"I don't know; you tell me."*

WHAT?

They thought this was a clever or humble answer. It wasn't. What it actually revealed was far more concerning.

It told me one of two things: either they didn't understand their own areas of contribution, or they believed deflecting the question would come across as humility.

In reality, it signaled a lack of self-awareness.

If a candidate can't articulate what they do well, it's unlikely they'll be able to add value at the level the role requires consistently.

Self-awareness isn't arrogance; it's clarity. And without it, impact becomes accidental rather than intentional.

Development Opportunities

These aren't weaknesses; they're opportunities for growth. A confident, self-aware person will be able to share where they need to improve. No one is perfect, so pretending otherwise signals either immaturity or a lack of humility.

Watch out for candidates who try to disguise a strength as a weakness. For instance, someone might say, "I'm overly dependable" or "I always get everything done no matter what." These statements often seem like a flaw, but are framed as a humble brag.

When I hear this, I ask:

"How does that impact the business or your team?"

If they can't give a real consequence, it's not truly a development opportunity.

Let's take the "I get everything done" example. I might follow up by asking:

- *"How do you prioritize tasks?"*

- *"How have you narrowed your team's focus when needed?"*

- *"Tell me about a time you were able to say no or delegate?"*

Often, that's when the candidate realizes their answer doesn't reflect true growth awareness.

The Overuse of Strengths

Many development areas stem from overusing a strength. Overuse happens when someone leans on their go-to behavior even when the situation calls for something different.

Here's a personal example:

I am highly structured, and I love a plan. But when things go off plan, my default response is to double down on more planning rather than pause and get curious about what's really going on. That's when I have to remind myself to *put the plan down and get curious.* The ability to recognize this before, or in the moment, is what self-awareness looks like in practice.

A truly self-aware candidate won't just tell you what they do; they'll explain why they do it. That's the gold standard.

Pre- and Post-Interview Discipline: Don't Skip the Steps

A structured approach before and after the interview isn't optional; it's essential.

Pre-Interview: Come Prepared

I was once invited to join an interview panel, only to be told after my interview that the decision had already been made. That's not just a waste of time; it's a sign of a broken process.

Before any interviews begin, the hiring team should be aligned on:

- The role and its expectations

- The competencies and behaviors being assessed

- Who is assessing what on the panel

Just as important: *do your homework*. Read the candidate's résumé before the interview so you can stay fully present and focused. Your job as an interviewer is to create the conditions for the candidate to show up authentically. If you're skimming a résumé during the conversation, you're already missing the mark.

Remember, your goal is to reduce bias.

Don't read other panelists' feedback before your interview.

Do form your own unbiased perspective to reduce groupthink and bias.

 *Storytime: Value Everyone's Perspective*

My team and I were interviewing for a director-level role. The interview schedule was set; everyone knew their role, and expectations were clear. Midway through the process, I checked in with the recruiters and learned that one interview recap was missing.

When I followed up, one of my direct reports told me he was waiting to submit his feedback until after I turned in mine.

No, sir.

I circled back immediately and said, "The reason you're part of this interview process is that I value your perspective. I don't need your feedback to align with mine; I need it to be yours."

That moment mattered. Waiting to mirror someone else's opinion undermines the entire purpose of having a panel. And misses out on important, intelligent perspectives needed to make the right decisions.

Groupthink has no place in interviews.

> **Lesson Learned:** If you want real insight, diverse perspectives, and better hiring decisions, you have to create space for independent judgment before selection decisions are made.

The recap is one of the most important sections in the interview process.

Don't skip the recap.

A structured post-interview recap is where the decision-making should happen, not before. If each interviewer assessed their assigned competencies and behaviors, your debrief will offer a well-rounded, accurate view of the candidate.

Skipping this step increases the risk of poor hiring decisions based on gut reactions or dominant voices in the room.

Watch Out: AI-Generated Interview Answers

I fully support candidates using AI to research a company, understand a role, or prepare for potential interview questions. That's thoughtful and resourceful preparation.

However, there's a big difference between *using* AI as a resource and *relying* on AI to generate their answers.

Let me give you an example. I once taught a workshop and asked AI to generate a list of the top three competencies for a director-level customer service role in the hospitality industry. I also asked for five great interview questions *and* ideal answers.

The room was amazed at what the platform produced: well-crafted questions *and* polished responses. The kind that could easily fool an undisciplined interviewer.

So, what do you do?

You probe. This is where AI ends, and authentic experience begins.

Probe questions force the candidate to go beyond the script. They reveal whether someone *actually lived* the experience they're describing, or if they're simply repeating something rehearsed.

This is how you shift from a performance to a conversation, one that surfaces real insight, depth, and fit.

Authenticity can't be copy-pasted. You've got to dig for it.

 ## Leadership Challenge: Competency Grid Activity

Take your organization's competencies and map out what overusing each behavior might look like.

You'll see an example of how I've done this using the **Coach Quen Competency Grid.** This exercise is a powerful way to surface the *dark side* of strengths, because every strength, when overused, can become a liability.

This grid helps leaders:

- **Assess** talent more accurately,

- **Develop** people with greater intention, and

- **Connect** behaviors to real-world impact on the team and business.

Understanding both the value and the risks of each competency leads to better coaching conversations and stronger leadership decisions.

 **Leadership Reflection:** Take a moment to reflect on how you overuse your strengths.

PARTIAL COMPETENCY GRID

Competencies	Behaviors	Overuse of Strengths
People Leadership: **Learner**	Seek Information Curious Listen Admit when wrong or need to change paths Self-reflective Self-developer	Delay in making a decision Stuck in learning/exploring Often question the direction May use hypotheticals "what if"
People Leadership: **Collaborator**	Build a strong network Leverage the network to drive results. Know when you need help and ask for it Inclusive Social	Don't act Request too much input Lack structure or routines
People Leadership: **Self-awareness (Know Yourself)**	Self reflect React to feedback Self control/composure Humble - Admit mistakes Know strengths and opportunities	Too tough on self Take blame Fail to assess others' role and hold them accountable
Thought Leadership: **Innovator/ Strategic**	Think in possibilities and big ideas Comfortable with ambiguity Break down steps to success Leverage data & internal/external influences	Never satisfied Miss or don't care about the details Not great at execution May get stuck in big picture
Thought Leadership: **Problem solver & Data-driven**	Critical thinker Understand process Leverage data Determined to reach a solution Quality decisions	Only see gaps Forget to celebrate wins Fixer May not collaborate to solve problems

Sources

Boyatzis, R. E. (2008). Competencies in the 21st century. *Journal of Management Development*, 27(1), 5–12.

Campion, M. A., Palmer, D. K., & Campion, J. E. (1997). A review of structure in the selection interview. *Personnel Psychology*, 50(3), 655–702.

Dipboye, R. L. (1994). *The selection interview: Process perspectives.* South-Western Publishing.

Janz, T. (1982). Initial comparisons of patterned behavior description interviews versus unstructured interviews. *Journal of Applied Psychology*, 67(5), 577–580.

Kaplan, R. E., & Kaiser, R. B. (2009). Stop overdoing your strengths. *Harvard Business Review*, 87(2), 100–103.

Levashina, J., Hartwell, C. J., Morgeson, F. P., & Campion, M. A. (2014). The structured employment interview. *Personnel Psychology*, 67(1), 241–293.

Spencer, L. M., & Spencer, S. M. (1993). *Competence at work: Models for superior performance.* Wiley.

Chapter Five

Intentional Match

As we wrap up this section, there are just a few other things to consider.

Make vs. Buy: Promote or Hire?

Another critical question: Should you *develop talent from within or hire externally?*

Coach Quen's Tip: If you're hiring externally, you should be buying capability, skills, experience, and leadership that immediately match the role's demands with a possibility for long-term potential. If you're ready to invest in someone's growth and long-term potential, promote from within, make the leader you want to see.

Don't hire an external project. If you want a strategic investment, make it an internal promotion. External talent needs to have the skills and capacity to do the job. They will need to learn the culture, build their network, and develop, but it should not be about teaching them how to do the job.

An internal hire already knows your culture, your people, and how to navigate your systems. They need development. An external hire needs to make an impact quickly.

You should always have a plan. One of the most important questions to answer is: What is the right talent mix for your department or organization to truly thrive?

External hires often bring fresh perspectives, new ideas, and experience gained outside your organization. Internal talent protects and strengthens your culture. These leaders already understand how the organization works, are bought into the mission and vision, and are invested in its success.

In organizations I've worked in, we used a *75/25 talent mix* as a guiding principle.

- 75% internal promotions required leaders to do their jobs well: selecting intentionally, developing consistently, and preparing high-potential talent for the next role.

- 25% external hires should be targeted, strategic additions who bring the skills, experience, and often the upward potential needed to elevate the business.

While this is a personal recommendation, this approach balanced continuity with innovation and ensured we weren't just filling roles; we were building a sustainable leadership pipeline.

Have a plan and choose intentionally. Don't pay to train someone you could have grown yourself.

 Leadership Challenge: Candidate Funnel - Are They a Match?

When you and your panel are engaging with a candidate, the **Coach Quen Candidate Funnel** helps you more easily assess fit for both the role and the broader organization. This framework provides clear checkpoints throughout the hiring journey to ensure alignment and intentionality in your assessment process.

There are five key areas of fit to evaluate. Use this five-stage funnel as a checklist during your post-interview debrief. Discuss each point with the panel and ensure there is alignment before making the final decision.

1. Mission & Values Fit

- Does the candidate demonstrate alignment with your organization's mission, purpose, and core values?

2. Core Role Capabilities

- Can the candidate successfully deliver the top 3 priorities required in the role?

- This isn't just about job titles, it's about core responsibilities and proven outcomes.

3. Relevant Experience

- Especially for external hires, are you "buying the experience"?

- Qualified candidates should bring experience that meaningfully contributes, often with upward potential.

- They should have been able to demonstrate this in the interview process.

4. Culture & Style Fit

- How do they work, lead, and collaborate?

- Are their behaviors, work style, and interpersonal dynamics compatible with your team's culture?

5. Desire Your Organization (or the role)

- Do they *truly want* to be a part of your company?

- *Avoid overselling the role or the company.* If you have to do all the convincing, ask yourself: "Do they really want to be here?"

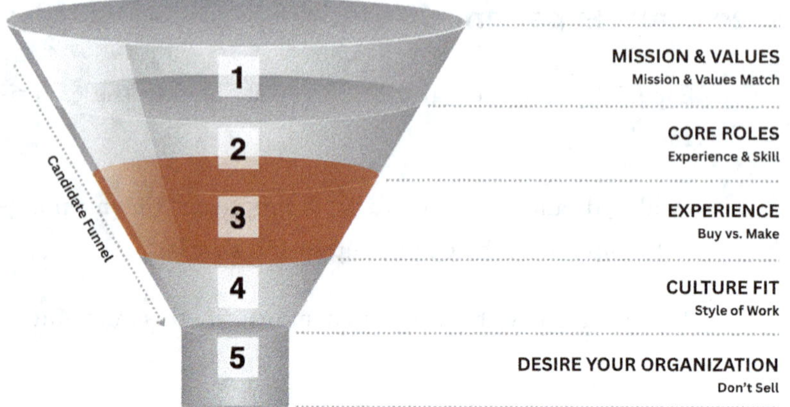

Coach Quen's Candidate Funnel

Assessment Tools

Assessment tools such as Hogan, Korn Ferry, DISC, and others are commonly used by organizations to evaluate talent fit. Whether to use these tools often comes down to organizational or leadership preference.

As a coach, I've chosen not to become certified in any specific assessment tool. That may change in the future and is not a judgment against coaches who are certified or organizations that use them; it's simply my preference. These tools provide useful data points to include in the total assessment. The key is understanding how to leverage these tools in the total assessment process.

In my experience, many of these tools get to the values of a person, and for professionals who have reached a certain level in their careers, these assessments often confirm what they already know. If you have to pick, I've found that a strong interview process, or in coaching, a well-facilitated values exercise, can reveal the same insights.

Additionally, many tools use proprietary languages that can be diffi-cult for candidates or leaders to recall or apply in practice. Whatever tool you use, it's essential to connect the language with the organi-zation's values and competencies rather than layering on an external language that might create confusion or disconnect.

Again, this comes down to organizational preference and resources. Whatever you decide to use, operationalize it and make it a part of the assessment process.

Hire Great, Never Just Good

One of the most important talent principles to remember: hire great, never good.

If you hire for great, even with the natural imperfections in any assessment process, the candidate may either live up to the high expectations or, at worst, perform at a solid level.

But if you hire for *good*, the candidate may only meet those average expectations, or worse, underperform.

Hiring high-performing talent protects your team, strengthens your organization, and drives results. Hiring someone who's just "good enough" comes with far greater risk:

Risk to morale, culture, and performance.

Aim high. Always.

Now that we know you have taken the time to intentionally match the talent to the organization, let's make sure they feel like they belong.

Sources

Bidwell, M. (2011). Paying more to get less: The effects of external hiring versus internal mobility. *Administrative Science Quarterly, 56*(3), 369–407.

Cappelli, P. (2008). *Talent on demand: Managing talent in an age of uncertainty.* Harvard Business School Press.

Chapman, D. S., Uggerslev, K. L., Carroll, S. A., Piasentin, K. A., & Jones, D. A. (2005). Applicant attraction to organizations and job choice. *Journal of Applied Psychology, 90*(5), 928–944.

Chatman, J. A. (1991). Matching people and organizations. *Academy of Management Journal, 34*(3), 459–484.

Highhouse, S. (2008). Stubborn reliance on intuition in employee selection. *Industrial and Organizational Psychology, 1*(3), 333–342.

Kristof-Brown, A. L., Zimmerman, R. D., & Johnson, E. C. (2005). Consequences of individuals' fit at work. *Personnel Psychology, 58*(2), 281–342.

Schmidt, F. L., & Hunter, J. E. (1998). The validity and utility of selection methods. *Psychological Bulletin, 124*(2), 262–274.

Spencer, L. M., & Spencer, S. M. (1993). *Competence at work: Models for superior performance.* Wiley.

PART III

BELONG
INTEGRATING FOR IMPACT

Belong

Talent doesn't perform at its highest level unless people feel they belong.

Hiring the right person is only the beginning; how they experience the team once they arrive determines whether they will truly contribute, grow, and stay.

Belonging creates the conditions for trust, engagement, and accountability, all of which directly influence performance.

When people feel seen, heard, and valued, they invest more deeply in the work and the success of the team. That is why belonging is not just a cultural concept, it is a leadership responsibility and a business advantage.

In this section, we will explore how leaders create the environment where talent can thrive.

Chapter Six

Onboarding with Intention

We often breathe a sigh of relief after hiring a new team member, especially one we're excited about. We put in the hard work to attract them, vet them, and make the final offer. But here's the truth:

The hardest work isn't behind you. It's ahead.

This is not the moment to step back. This is when you lean in.

Orientation vs. Onboarding

Onboarding is the first 30, 60, and 90 days of someone's new role. Orientation is one part of onboarding. It is usually the first day or introduction to the new gig.

Orientation is a one-time, short-term event.

The purpose is to introduce new hires to the essential information they need to get started. That includes:

- Completing required paperwork

- Understanding company policies

- Reviewing benefits

- Receiving tools like badges, laptops, or a tour of the work-space

Typically led by HR, orientation ensures employees are set up logistically, but this is *not* a moment for hiring leaders to disengage.

Your involvement matters!

You might ask your new talent:

- "Do you have any questions about the policies or benefits HR reviewed with you?"

- "Was there anything missing or unclear during your orientation?"

- "Jot down anything that comes up over your first 30 days; we'll revisit and address what we missed."

From the beginning, you must be engaged with your talent.

The longer play is onboarding. This is a strategic, long-term process designed to:

- Integrate new employees into the culture

- Build connections with people and processes

- Clarify expectations and workflows

- Build competence and confidence in the role

- Accelerate time to performance

Onboarding is where *belonging* is built.

Unfortunately, many organizations reduce onboarding to a few administrative steps or skip it entirely.

That could be a big miss.

The faster someone feels like they *belong*, the sooner they can contribute meaningfully.

Oh, and by the way, this isn't just the leader's responsibility; it's the whole team's job.

Belonging is a Team Sport

Your team should be aligned on who's responsible for each part of welcoming and integrating the new hire. Don't assume this will happen organically.

Peers play a critical role. A great peer:

- Introduces the new hire to their network

- Explains cultural norms (spoken and unspoken)

- Models team routines

- Shares insights like, "Here's how our boss communicates best."

These peer actions are *vital*. Without them, new hires waste energy interpreting signals, second-guessing their behavior, or wondering if they fit in.

If someone is constantly thinking, *"What did that mean?"*, they're not fully focused on learning the role or delivering results.

A Word of Caution

Orientation and Onboarding are not:

- Handing over a binder from the last person who had the job

- Hoping they "figure it out"

- Delegating everything to HR

It is about creating an environment where someone feels integrated, engaged, and clear about what's expected.

A thoughtful onboarding experience helps new hires feel connected, aligned, confident, and ready to thrive.

📖 Storytime: It Starts Day One

Being a new hire can feel a lot like being the new kid in junior high; you just want the cool kids to like you.

I remember starting a new role at an organization and feeling that familiar first-day nervousness. Simple questions raced through my mind:

How will I know where the bathroom is?

Who will I sit with at lunch?

But what I remember most clearly is the moment my boss met me at the door. She personally walked me into the building, sat with me to outline what my day and week would look like, and even though she handed me off to HR for the paperwork, she made a point to check in throughout the day. She even made sure we had lunch together with the entire team.

That's leadership presence.

That might sound like a small gesture, maybe even a low bar, but here's the truth: not one other company or department had ever done that for me. And this was after I had reached a director-level role. Multiple positions, several promotions, and still, no one had taken that kind of time, intention, or care.

By the end of the day, I didn't just know where to find the bathroom. I knew what my week would look like; I felt seen, supported, and accepted, and yes, I had a place to sit at lunch. That's what a thoughtful start to an onboarding experience looks like. And it matters more than most leaders realize.

Lesson Learned: Belonging starts on day one. What is your plan for a successful start?

Leadership Challenge

Ask yourself, what is happening on day one for our new hires? If you don't know the answer, it's time to dig in.

Leadership Challenge: 30-60-90 Day Plan

Work with your new hire to map out a strategy from Day 1 to Day 90. This is especially useful for leadership roles.

- First 30 Days: Learn the culture, meet key stakeholders, observe and assess the wins and gaps, and ask questions.

- Days 31–60: Begin contributing to early wins, shadow workflows, and refine focus areas.

- Days 61–90: Drive independent outcomes, share feedback, and co-create development goals.

Many leaders say, *"I don't have time to do this."*

They are right; I have never met a leader who said, "I have so much time, I don't know what I'm going to do with myself."

But I don't think we have the luxury of not?

Every action you take as a leader either accelerates progress and results or slows them down. There is no neutrality.

So the real question is: *Which one are you choosing?*

Onboarding is the first step to building psychological safety. Let's explore this concept more in the next chapter.

Sources

Baumeister, R. F., & Leary, M. R. (1995). The need to belong. Psychological Bulletin, 117(3), 497–529.

Bauer, T. N. (2010). Onboarding new employees: Maximizing success. SHRM Foundation.

Edmondson, A. (1999). Psychological safety and learning behavior in work teams. Administrative Science Quarterly, 44(2), 350–383.

Kahn, R. L., Wolfe, D. M., Quinn, R. P., Snoek, J., & Rosenthal, R. (1964). Organizational stress: Studies in role conflict and ambiguity. Wiley.

Van Maanen, J., & Schein, E. H. (1979). Toward a theory of organizational socialization. Research in Organizational Behavior, 1, 209–264.

Watkins, M. (2013). The first 90 days: Proven strategies for getting up to speed faster and smarter. Harvard Business Review Press.

Chapter Seven

Building Psychological Safety and Belonging

Trust, Safety, and Connection = Performance Multipliers

What does that mean?

It means when you create a culture where people feel safe, connected, and trusted, you unlock performance and accelerate results.

If you've ever heard of *cognitive overload*, you know it's when someone's brain is so overwhelmed that they can't operate at full capacity.

It's like when a hungry child struggles to learn because their basic needs aren't met. They are worried about their next meal, not the math problem on the board. Adults are no different.

When someone feels anxious, disconnected, or unsafe, especially in a new environment, they shift into survival mode. Creativity, learning, and performance shut down. And you're left wondering,

Where is the person I hired?

They're in there. But without an environment of trust and safety, they can't show up fully.

The leader must create this environment of trust and safety to inspire greatness.

Inclusion, Trust, and Team Norms

Inclusion isn't a program; it's a way of being.

Inclusion is where every individual feels empowered to contribute. It's not just about who's in the room; it's about how people feel once they're there.

Where diversity focuses on representation, inclusion focuses on experience.

Inclusive environments are:

- **Psychologically Safe** – People feel comfortable being themselves without fear of judgment or penalty.

- **Equitable** – Everyone has fair access to opportunities, resources, and advancement.

- **Engaging** – People are invited to contribute and influence outcomes.

When people feel seen, heard, and valued, they bring their best.

Inclusion fuels engagement, innovation, trust, and team performance.

Leaders Create the Climate

It is the leader's responsibility to build an inclusive, trust-based environment. One way to start?

Team norms.

In my first book, *The Accountability Advantage*, I shared an activity called *Rules of Engagement*. This is where the team co-creates how they want to work together, how they show up, communicate, and hold each other accountable.

These aren't just warm-and-fuzzy ideas. Clear norms help people:

- Understand what's expected

- Know what's acceptable

- Feel safe holding others accountable

📖 Storytime: The Power of Ownership Norms

I always say, "I'll tell you when I'm going to tell ON you." Sounds funny, but it's real. When I was a business partner visiting a struggling store, I would work alongside the leaders, help them identify the issue, and create a plan forward. Then I'd say, "You need to call your boss, because I'm updating them in an hour." Why? Because it's always better coming from you than from me.

That was our norm. Own your stuff. Don't make someone else play the snitch.

Even when I was a young coach for a high school cheerleading team, I told my team, "Everyone makes mistakes." Just don't let me hear about it from someone else. You'd better tell me.

Lesson Learned: I may have been early in my leadership journey, but I knew then what I teach now: accountability and trust are foundational to team culture.

Let People Be Seen, Heard, and Safe

Creating psychological safety does *not* mean lowering standards or avoiding accountability. It means creating the *conditions* where accountability can actually exist.

It's about building a team where:

- People don't feel the need to hide.

- Mistakes can be acknowledged, learned from, and corrected.

- Everyone understands what the team stands for and what behaviors won't fly.

When people truly feel like they belong, they stop operating in survival mode and start *thriving*.

So, how do you create this as a leader? One step is to respond versus react.

Respond - Don't React

One of the most powerful ways leaders build psychological safety is by choosing to respond rather than react.

Reacting is immediate and emotional. Something happens, and the reaction comes straight from instinct. Sometimes that reaction lands well, but other times, it's exactly what you wish you hadn't said five seconds later. Reaction is fast, but often unfiltered.

Responding is different.

Responding means something happens, and you take a brief pause, just a few seconds, to process, consider the impact, and choose your words intentionally. This isn't about waiting an hour or avoiding the issue. It's about slowing down *just enough* to lead with clarity instead of emotion.

Responding still happens quickly, but it's *thoughtful, purposeful, and adaptive.*

When you respond, you can meet the moment with what it actually needs: guidance, accountability, curiosity, or support, rather than escalating tension or shutting people down.

And when leaders respond with intention, teams learn it's safe to speak up, take ownership, and grow.

That's how belonging is built.
That's how trust is earned.
And that's how performance follows.

🏔 Leadership Challenge

Coach Quen's Checklist for Building Psychological Safety & Belonging

Use the checklist in Chapter 14 to assess your team's current environment and take action to strengthen belonging, trust, and inclusion.

Sources

Edmondson, A. (1999). Psychological safety and learning behavior in work teams. *Administrative Science Quarterly, 44*(2), 350–383.

Hackman, J. R. (2002). *Leading teams: Setting the stage for great performances.* Harvard Business School Press.

Rozovsky, J. (2015). *The five keys to a successful Google team.* Google re: Work.

Schneider, B., Ehrhart, M. G., & Macey, W. H. (2013). Organizational climate and culture. *Annual Review of Psychology, 64*, 361–388.

Chapter Eight

The Power of Identity and Inclusion

By now, you know that inclusion is essential to creating a strong team culture.

But here's the key insight: *one of the most powerful ways to foster inclusion is by helping someone build a sense of identity and self-efficacy.*

When people believe they can contribute meaningfully, they begin to see themselves as valued members of the team, and that's when belonging truly takes root.

Self-Efficacy vs. Confidence: What's the Difference?

Self-efficacy is the belief in your ability to successfully perform specific tasks or achieve particular goals in a given situation. Psychologist Albert Bandura introduced the term, which is both task-specific and contextual.

Example: "I believe I can lead this team through a difficult transition because I've done it before and I know what it takes."

It's influenced by:

- Past successes or failures

- Observing others' success (vicarious learning)

- Encouragement from others (social persuasion)

- Your emotional state (e.g., stress or anxiety can lower efficacy)

Confidence, on the other hand, is a broader, more general belief in yourself and your abilities.

Example: "I'm confident in my leadership skills overall."

While confidence can exist even when you're trying something new, *self-efficacy grows through experience and success in a specific area.*

Leaders must nurture self-efficacy to help team members thrive. When it fades, performance often declines with it.

SELF-EFFICACY AND CONFIDENCE KEY DIFFERENCES

Aspect	Self-Efficacy	Confidence
Definition	Belief in the ability to succeed at a specific task	General belief in oneself or abilities
Scope	Task- and situation-specific	Broad and general
Origin	Developed through mastery, observation, feedback, and emotion	Can stem from personality, experience, or mindset
Impact on Behavior	Strong predictor of motivation and performance in specific situations	Influences attitude and overall presence
Example	"I can deliver this keynote speech."	"I'm a good public speaker."

Knowing Your Role Drives Engagement and Identity

We've already talked about the importance of role clarity in doing a great job, but it's also about identity.

People need to understand:

- What they do

- Why it matters

- How it connects to the team's success

That's how identity is formed, when someone can say, *"This is the value I bring to this team."*

Training Is the Foundation

More often than not, when someone is hired, the role has already been vacant, and their talents are needed immediately. Leaders rarely have the luxury of a perfectly timed transition, where the outgoing leader overlaps with the new hire and provides ample time for a smooth handoff.

But here's the truth: ***training cannot be skipped.***

Even when timelines are tight, leaders must get creative to ensure new hires receive the foundational training they need to feel effective and capable in their roles. Without it, you are setting them and the business up for unnecessary struggle.

Time is rarely on our side. But when we shortcut foundational training, we inevitably spend far more time on the back end fixing preventable mistakes.

Not everything needs to be mastered on day one. Some skills can absolutely be learned along the journey. But the fundamentals, the core responsibilities, expectations, systems, and decision-making levers, must be solid.

Because when the foundation is strong, performance accelerates. When it's weak, there is no stability.

Helping People Understand Why They're Valued

One of the fastest ways to build identity is to make it crystal clear why someone is valued.

Here's how:

- **Representation matters**: When people see others like them in meaningful roles, they know they belong.

- **Voice matters**: When people are asked to share ideas or lead initiatives, they see the impact of their work.

- **Recognition matters**: When people are acknowledged for their unique strengths, they feel seen.

📖 Storytime: Power of Team Values & Identity

I once led a team of four with very different working styles. To build our team identity, I facilitated a values workshop. Each person identified what mattered most to them:

- *Two team members valued process and working methodically.*

- *One valued speed, moving fast to find solutions.*

- *One valued collaboration and harmony.*

By the end of the session, everyone had a clear identity on the team. And more importantly, we gave each other permission to play our roles fully.

- *The "speed" person could say, "Let's wrap this up in 10 minutes."*

- *The "process" folks could say, "We need to spend more time here; this is high stakes."*

- *The "collaborator" could step in when we started drifting apart.*

We honored each other's values, and we played to our strengths. That's what belonging looks like.

Inclusion and Belonging - Why People Stay

People stay when they feel:

- They have an identity on the team

- They are contributing in meaningful ways

- They trust and believe in their leadership

Those are the cornerstones of *trust, inclusion, and belonging.*

Leadership Reflection: Building Identity and Belonging

This exercise helps you reflect on how, as a leader or team member, you foster identity, inclusion, and self-efficacy within your team. It invites you to assess how intentionally you're creating an environment where people feel seen, valued, and empowered to play their role.

Part 1: Personal Reflection

1. When did I first feel like I truly belonged on a team?

- *What helped me feel that way?*

- *Who contributed to that experience?*

2. Think about a current or past team member:

- *Do they know why they are valued on the team?*

- *Have I communicated their strengths or unique contributions to them?*

3. How do I currently support someone's self-efficacy?

- *When was the last time I acknowledged someone's growth or potential?*

- *Do I give people "permission" to lean into their strengths?*

Part 2: Identity Mapping

For each of your direct reports or close team members, list:

- **Their superpower** *(a unique trait or strength)*

- **How it helps the team succeed**

- **How they might overuse it**

- **Whether they know this is their value**

Then reflect:

- *Do they feel seen for this contribution?*

- *Do we make space for them to use this strength fully?*

- *How can I help them refine it and grow?*

Part 3: Team Dialogue

Use one of the following prompts in your next 1:1 or team meeting:

- *"What part of the team's success do you feel most connected to?"*

- *"What's one strength you wish we relied on more from you?"*

- *"What's one way we can help each other feel more included and valued?"*

Final Journal Prompt:

Reflect: What am I doing as a leader or peer to make this true?

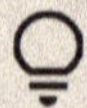

Coach Quen's Tip: People stay where they feel seen, where they can contribute, and where they trust the leadership.

Sources

Bandura, A. (1997). *Self-efficacy: The exercise of control.* W. H. Freeman.

Baumeister, R. F., & Leary, M. R. (1995). The need to belong. *Psychological Bulletin, 117*(3), 497–529.

Harter, J. K., Schmidt, F. L., & Hayes, T. L. (2002). Business-unit-level relationship between employee satisfaction and business outcomes. *Journal of Applied Psychology, 87*(2), 268–279.

Kahn, R. L., Wolfe, D. M., Quinn, R. P., Snoek, J., & Rosenthal, R. (1964). *Organizational stress: Studies in role conflict and ambiguity.* Wiley.

Rizzo, J. R., House, R. J., & Lirtzman, S. I. (1970). Role conflict and ambiguity in complex organizations. *Administrative Science Quarterly, 15*(2), 150–163.

Salas, E., Tannenbaum, S. I., Kraiger, K., & Smith-Jentsch, K. A. (2012). The science of training and development. *Psychological Science in the Public Interest, 13*(2), 74–101.

Stajkovic, A. D., & Luthans, F. (1998). Self-efficacy and work-related performance. *Psychological Bulletin, 124*(2), 240–261.

PART IV

DEVELOP

FROM NEW HIRE TO HIGH PERFORMER

Develop

Development is one of the most important responsibilities a leader holds, because when you grow your people, you grow your business. And yet, despite its importance, many leaders struggle with the *how*. They know development matters, but they lack the tools, structure, or confidence to do it well.

In this section, we'll explore the mindset and methods of high-impact development, and give you specific, actionable strategies to help build a team that doesn't just perform, but thrives.

Chapter Nine

Grow the Person, Grow the Business

The first step in developing people is clarity.

You must be *specific*, specific about expectations, goals, behaviors, and what success looks like. Great performance doesn't come from assumption or guesswork. It comes from alignment.

Too often, we fall into the trap of thinking:

> "This person is amazing. I don't need to do much; they'll figure it out."

That mindset can create confusion, drift, and underperformance. Even top talent needs direction, feedback, and attention. *Most people aren't, "just add water".* They need thoughtful guidance to reach their full potential.

That's why great leadership requires more than just managing. It requires *coaching*.

It means knowing when to give direction, and when to step back. When to challenge and when to support. When to zoom in with clarity, and when to zoom out to let them lead.

Because when you invest in the person, you elevate the performance.

📖 Storytime: Everyone Needs Leadership

A great example comes from an organization where I worked alongside some of the most brilliant people I've ever encountered. These were exceptionally smart, creative thinkers. I could ask a question, and they'd come back with an answer that completely reframed the problem. I remember calling a friend just to brag about the level of talent on that team.

And yet, even with all that brilliance, they still needed time and attention.

No one had ever taught them business acumen. They had a powerful vision but struggled to operationalize it. They didn't yet understand which business levers to pull to translate ideas into results.

That team taught me something important: intelligence alone isn't enough. Even the brightest talent needs both coaching and managing to turn insight into impact.

Lesson Learned: It was a joy to lead that team because I learned to balance my time between coaching and managing, and when leaders meet talent where they are, genuine progress happens.

Let's look at the difference between coaching and managing.

Coaching and Managing

Coaching is a *development-focused* approach centered on unlocking a person's potential, helping them grow, and guiding them to discover their own solutions.

> **Coaching is the intentional act of helping someone think, grow, and act with clarity by asking the right questions rather than giving all the answers. It's about unlocking self-awareness, guiding growth, and knowing when to get closer so you can confidently step back.**

Great coaches create space for others to find their own path, while staying close enough to support progress and course-correct when needed. It's a balance of presence and permission.

Coaching is built on trust, curiosity, and empowerment. It's a conversation, not a directive. It helps people reflect, expand their thinking, and take ownership of their learning.

Equally important, managing is a *performance-focused* role that ensures tasks are completed, goals are met, and team operations run effectively. It involves setting expectations, assigning work, providing direction, and holding people accountable.

> **Managing is about aligning people and resources to achieve business results. It's about clarity, accountability, and execution.**

KEY DIFFERENCES: COACHING VS. MANAGING

Aspect	Coaching	Managing
Focus	Growth and development	Performance and delivery
Approach	Ask questions to guide	Give direction to act
Timeframe	Long-term potential	Short- to mid-term outcomes
Style	Empowerment, listening	Directing, monitoring
Goal	Unlock self-awareness and ownership	Drive consistency and results
Tone	Curious and supportive	Clear and accountable
Example	"What's getting in your way?"	"This task is due by Friday."

Self-Awareness and Team Awareness

If you and your team aren't regularly talking about strengths, development areas, triggers, and the overuse of natural talents, that's the first place to start.

Self-awareness isn't optional for high-performing teams; it's foundational.

Building a culture of self-awareness enables individuals to better understand how they show up, how others experience them, and how their behaviors impact team dynamics. When teams normalize conversations around behavior and mindset, they unlock a culture of *self-monitoring, self-correction, and peer accountability.*

The Definitions

- **Self-Monitoring:** Each person pays attention to their own behavior and asks: *"Is how I'm showing up helping or hurting the team right now?"*

- **Self-Correction:** Individuals take responsibility for shifting their behavior, in the moment, to better align with the team's values and culture.

- **Team Accountability:** The team holds each other accountable to shared norms proactively, consistently, and with care.

Why It Matters

When people understand their default behaviors, especially under stress or pressure, they can catch themselves before those behaviors become a barrier. And when teammates feel safe to call each other in, not out, that's where real accountability starts.

Self-awareness leads to emotional intelligence.

Emotional intelligence leads to trust.

Trust leads to performance.

Coach Quen's Tip: In *The Accountability Advantage*, I introduced a *values exercise* for teams. It's a powerful first step toward building self-awareness and aligning team behaviors. Use it early and revisit it often. It's not a one-time conversation; it's the foundation for a culture where people know their strengths, own their impact, and grow together.

Feedback and Development Plans

Feedback should be a *routine*, not a surprise. It should happen during 1:1s, in real time, after key meetings, and following moments of impact, both positive and constructive. People should expect feedback. It's how growth becomes part of the culture.

I remember a boss once told me, *"You're easy to give feedback to."* I laughed and said, *"That's because I've already given myself the feedback before your name even pops up on my phone."*

Let's be honest, feedback doesn't always feel good. It still doesn't feel good to me. But in the second half of my career, I had developed enough self-awareness to know when I had missed the mark. I didn't need someone else to point it out for me to feel the sting. That's the kind of self-monitoring we want to cultivate on our teams.

📖 *Storytime: Self-Awareness and Authenticity*

Like many organizations, we had a high-potential program in which leaders took part in an assessment process designed to clarify their strengths, identify gaps, and prepare them for future roles.

One store manager I was coaching through the process came to meet with me to make sure she was ready to tell her story. She walked into my office looking panicked, clutching a notebook, and sat down at the table. As she started talking, I barely recognized her.

I asked simple questions:
"What are you most proud of?"
"What have you accomplished in your building?"

Instead of answering naturally, she flipped through her notes, searching for the "right" response to experiences she had lived. I finally stopped her and said,
"Who is this sitting in front of me? I don't know who you are, and I don't want to talk to you. I want to talk to the person I usually interact with."

Then I told her to leave and only come back when she was ready to be herself.

She stood up and walked out to the bathroom.
Ten minutes passed.
Then fifteen.

I panicked. Did I push too hard?
Do I need to go find her and talk her down?

Just as I stepped into the hallway, she walked back toward me. She entered my office and sat down, this time without the notebook.

I asked, "Are you good?"
She smiled and said, "Absolutely."

What followed was one of the best conversations we had ever had. She spoke confidently about her focus, her accomplishments, and her areas for growth. She was thoughtful, self-aware, and authentic.

She became the top candidate in the assessment process, just as I knew she could be. And as I have kept track of her career, she was recently promoted to vice president. Of course she was!

Lesson Learned: Here's what that experience reinforced for me...I will take the authentic leader every day of the week over the rehearsed one, trying to say what they think I want to hear. Authenticity signals that the real work has already been done: the development, the feedback, and the self-awareness.

And that leader will always outperform the "what I should say" version.

The Power of Individual Development Plans (IDPs)

One of the most underutilized tools in leadership development is the Individual Development Plan (IDP). These are not HR check-the-box forms; they are strategic tools to drive growth, alignment, and accountability.

When created and used correctly, an IDP connects individual goals to team and business goals, leadership competencies, and long-term aspirations.

Let me give you an example:

When I was new to an organization, I asked a skip-level leader about her IDP. She smiled and said, *"I don't have one, but I can share my goals."*

Her number one goal? *"Go to Paris."*

Now listen, I'm all for Paris. But that goal wasn't aligned with what the business needed, and it highlighted something important:

> **Don't assume people know how to build a great development plan.**

Even strong, experienced leaders often need guidance and input.

What Makes a Strong IDP?

An effective IDP is a *shared responsibility* between the employee and the leader.

- **The individual owns** the plan. They identify growth areas, connect them to feedback and competency expectations, and propose development actions.

- **The leader guides and supports** the plan. They offer honest feedback, ensure focus areas are relevant, and stay close enough to track progress and offer course corrections.

This isn't a "once-a-year" document. It's a *living plan* that should evolve as the person grows and business needs shift.

If you and your team don't have **active** Individual Development Plans, make this a *top priority, right alongside building self-awareness.* Together, these two form the foundation for sustainable growth and high performance.

No Surprises: Making Reviews a Reinforcement Tool

I won't spend too much time on review processes because every organization handles them differently. Some conduct reviews twice a year; others do them quarterly. Some use detailed evaluation forms with multiple sections, while others rely on just a few key questions.

Regardless of the format, the most important principle remains the same:

Performance reviews should never be a surprise.

Not the content.
Not the tone.
Not the wording.

Reviews are not the time to introduce new information. They are the time to reinforce what has already been discussed, coached, and aligned on throughout the year.

The review process should underscore the messages that have consistently been communicated. It should reflect ongoing feedback, not replace it.

If your team frequently seems surprised during performance reviews, that's not a review problem; it's a feedback problem. Go back and evaluate how often, how clearly, and how directly you're giving feedback in real time.

One powerful alignment tool is the *self-review*. Asking individuals to assess their own performance before the formal review gives you valuable insight. It allows you to see whether expectations have been understood, absorbed, and owned. When there's alignment between the self-review and your assessment, you know the communication has landed. When there's a gap, you've identified a clarity opportunity.

Reviews shouldn't be events.
They should be confirmations.

Let People Enjoy the Learning Journey

Development isn't about perfection. It's about progress.
And progress is often messy.

📖 *Storytime: The Three-Day Spiral*

Let me tell you a story from my coaching certification training.
I was so eager to get it right that I forgot the most important part: you're not supposed to be perfect when you're learning.

During my first recorded practice session with a client, I was terrible. I over-directed, talked too much, and steamrolled my client. When I had to listen to the recording with my mentor, I nearly melted into the floor. After the call, I spiraled...

for three whole days.

It took me that long to ask myself one simple question:
"Why did I expect to be great at something I had never done before?"

I had been so focused on performing that I wasn't giving myself the space to learn.

That moment changed how I view development.

Lesson Learned: Leave space for learning.

What Does This Mean for Your Team?

Ask yourself:

- Are you giving your team space to make mistakes and recover?

- Are you normalizing feedback and learning as part of your culture?

- Or are you creating a climate where people spiral instead of grow?

No one *likes* making mistakes. But when mistakes happen, your *reaction* sets the tone:

1. Do you lead them into a shame spiral?

2. Or do you help them shift quickly to reflection and action?

The faster you can move from "what went wrong" to "what did we learn", the faster your people and your business will grow.

Now let's get into some development specifics to help you move from development to advancement.

Sources

Boyatzis, R. E., & McKee, A. (2005). *Resonant leadership.* Harvard Business School Press.

Day, D. V. (2001). Leadership development: A review in context. *Leadership Quarterly, 11*(4), 581–613.

Goleman, D. (1995). *Emotional intelligence: Why it can matter more than IQ.* Bantam Books.

Goleman, D. (2000). Leadership that gets results. *Harvard Business Review, 78*(2), 78–90.

Kluger, A. N., & DeNisi, A. (1996). The effects of feedback interventions on performance. *Psychological Bulletin, 119*(2), 254–284.

London, M. (2003). *Job feedback: Giving, seeking, and using feedback for performance improvement.* Lawrence Erlbaum.

McCauley, C. D., & Van Velsor, E. (2004). *The Center for Creative Leadership handbook of leadership development.* Jossey-Bass.

Whitmore, J. (2017). *Coaching for performance* (5th ed.). Nicholas Brealey.

Chapter Ten

Development Tactics

In my first book, *The Accountability Advantage*, I introduced the concept that before you can hold your team accountable, you must first own your role as a leader. Development starts with you.

I also shared the ***Development & Feedback Escalation Map,*** a tool to guide your actions when growth stalls or performance slips. The core principle remains the same:

> **If development and results aren't moving, the leader must do something different.**

The overview of this map on the next page helps you take intentional action based on the *issue's impact or frequency*, not just how frustrated you feel in the moment. It provides a structure for your leadership response so you don't underreact, overreact, or miss a growth opportunity.

It helps you develop your team.

Let's revisit the map and lean more into the *leadership actions* associated with each step.

DEVELOPMENT AND FEEDBACK MAP

Occurrence	Example Situation	Leadership Action
First	Team member misses a deadline	Clarify the expectation & reset support
Second	Pattern repeats	Have a direct conversation about impact & accountability. Get closer to the business and the leader.
Third	Still no shift	Escalate - align on consequence with performance improvement plans

Clarify the Expectation

By now, expectations, roles, and responsibilities should be clear. But when something slips, don't assume the person *knows* what was expected; check for understanding.

- Reconfirm timelines, priorities, and quality expectations.

- Ask, *"Where did we miss?"* and *"What do you need from me to succeed?"*

- Use curiosity, not frustration.

This is also the time to *reset your support*. If tools, clarity, or feedback loops are needed, now's the time to get that in place.

Get Closer

When additional development is needed on the same issue or behavior, it's time to get closer, specifically, closer to the leader and the business.

Some may confuse this with micromanagement, but let's be clear:

Micromanagement is forcing someone to do it your way. Getting closer is leadership.

You're not taking over, you're leaning in with intention.

Getting closer can take many forms:

- Observing behavior in action

- Sitting in on decision-making moments

- Shadowing conversations

- Raising the frequency and depth of your coaching touchpoints

It's not about control, it's about proximity.
It's about understanding what's missing so you can coach more effectively and accelerate growth.

Shadow the Leader

Whether you're shadowing them or they're shadowing you, the goal is the same: to uncover gaps in understanding, observe habits, and identify where development is needed.

I used this often when I joined a new team. We'd always start by aligning on key expectations, such as our definition of top talent, our interview process, and what makes a candidate successful. Once those standards were clear, if the next couple of candidates I interviewed didn't hit the mark, it was time to shadow the leader.

Here's how I did it:

- The leader would interview their candidate first.

- Then, they'd join my interview with the same candidate.

- Afterward, we'd debrief on what they noticed, learned, and might improve in their approach.

One example: many leaders conduct interviews on the move. Seems simple, but it shows something critical: *they aren't protecting the time or creating the space to be fully present.* As a result, they may miss important cues and insights from candidates. You may only learn about this gap by shadowing and asking questions.

This process works in reverse, too. You can observe the leader first *after* you've demonstrated the expectation. Think of it as *"show and tell", then observe and adjust.* Teach first, then shadow to ensure the lesson sticks.

The goal isn't to shame. It's about getting close enough to understand where growth needs to happen and to support it intentionally.

Increase Check-Ins

Increasing the number of check-ins is one of the most effective ways to get closer to the work and to your people.

You should never wait until a project is due to check on progress. When expectations aren't met, it's a signal that milestone check-ins should happen more frequently. If you're used to holding 1:1s every other week, consider shifting to *weekly* until consistency returns.

For projects that are slipping or team members who need more development, a simple 10-minute check-in every Friday can be transformational. It doesn't require much time, but it *keeps things on track,* provides space for clarification, and helps you step in quickly when support or redirection is needed.

It's not about micromanaging; it's about showing you're invested, paying attention, and creating enough touchpoints to drive accountability and growth.

One note: There should be a sunset on having increased check-ins. If the person's performance depends on your check-ins, different actions may be needed.

Increase Structured Feedback

Adding more structured feedback can be a game-changer, especially for teams operating in informal cultures. In informal environments, feedback can feel casual or vague. What you see as a serious issue might come across to others as *"not a big deal".*

That's where structure makes the difference.

A simple yet effective tactic is to ask the team member to send a recap email after a key meeting or conversation. This isn't about writing a report; it's about:

- Clarifying what they heard

- What they plan to do

- And by when

Just a few bullet points can tell you everything you need to know about how aligned (or misaligned) you are.

This is especially important if you're concerned about someone's understanding of expectations, priorities, or timelines. Having *them* do the recap is more telling than you doing it for them. Why? Because you already know what was said, what you need to know is what they actually heard.

Yes, it can work when the leader sends the recap, but if you're past the point of restating expectations, it's time to assess comprehension. Having them take the lead gives you insight into what's landing and what's not.

Structured feedback is about clarity. But it will also be needed if you need to escalate performance management.

Increase Structured Follow-Up

Follow-up doesn't have to feel formal; it can be fun, creative, and effective, especially when it visibly reinforces accountability.

Structured follow-up can include:

- Sending photos of completed work

- Setting calendar due dates with reminders

- Sharing quick progress reports or "proof of completion" recaps

When I worked in retail and hospitality, I'd often ask leaders to email me a photo of the section they'd fixed, along with a brief note explaining what they'd corrected and how they'd adjusted their routines so the issue wouldn't happen again. It wasn't just about the fix; it was about learning and improvement.

I'd also challenge leaders to email me when they hit a milestone, but with a twist:
The subject line had to be something bold and catchy, like *"How You Like Me Now"* or *"Boom"*.

Why?

Because I get hundreds of emails a day. If I saw that title, I'd drop everything to open it and celebrate with them. It made accountability feel rewarding, not robotic.

For shared calendar invites for due dates, I'd say:

> *"That reminder will either be a good ding if you hit the goal, or a bad ding if you didn't. Just don't have me be the one to ask, because you know it dinged on my side also."*

It was light-hearted, but it made expectations clear.

Bottom line: Structured follow-up gives you proof of progress, sustains momentum, and reminds people *you're paying attention*. And sometimes, that's all they need to step up.

Focus Calls

Focus calls should be used sparingly and only when something isn't moving or has clearly gone off the rails. These meetings often involve multiple people and require a significant investment of time, so they must be purposeful and well-structured.

When used correctly, focus calls can be very impactful. But if they are not handled carefully, they can unintentionally strip ownership away from the leaders who are supposed to be accountable for the results.

When I stepped into a new leadership role, I inherited a team that was already on recurring focus calls. The business results were off track, key performance indicators were being missed, and senior leaders were joining these calls every month. It didn't take long for me to realize that this approach wasn't sustainable or productive.

My first goal was simple: *get my team off those calls.*

Why? Because I was the leader responsible for their development and their results. I didn't need two or three levels above me managing my team; I needed to own it.

My second goal was to demonstrate that I was in the details and actively moving the business forward. In every organization, there are a few key metrics that serve as leading indicators. When those start moving in the right direction, they signal that the root problems are being addressed. Those were the measurements I focused on improving first.

My final goal was to secure the support the team needed, but in the right way, not through a standing monthly call. In this situation, there were specific resources and support mechanisms the team needed in order to succeed. Once I had established credibility by moving results, I was ready with a clear list of requests.

Focus calls should be treated as *temporary interventions*, not long-term operating routines. Their purpose is to stabilize performance, restore ownership, and return accountability to the leaders closest to the work.

If You Use Focus Calls, Be Intentional:

- Clarify the purpose: What specific problem is this call solving?

- Define the audience: Who needs to be in the room, and who doesn't?

- Protect ownership: The appropriate leader should drive the conversation, not be managed by others.

- Outline follow-through: What are the next steps, and how will progress be monitored?

When done well, focus calls can bring urgency, visibility, and alignment. But without clarity and boundaries, they become a crutch that stalls true accountability.

Performance Improvement Plans (PIPs)

While Performance Improvement Plans (PIPs) are often viewed as a step toward managing someone out of the organization, the name itself tells us their true purpose: *improvement.*

A PIP is often one of the last steps in the development process, but the goal should be developmental. A key point is that performance is different from conduct. Performance is about ability; conduct is about choice. Trying to coach poor conduct will probably only prolong the issue. A PIP should not be used for conduct issues.

Performance issues are typically addressed through coaching, development, training, feedback, and structured improvement plans such as a PIP.

Conduct, on the other hand, refers to behavior and adherence to organizational standards, policies, and values. Conduct issues occur when someone violates expected workplace behavior or company policies.

The intent of the PIP is to provide the individual with a structured opportunity to correct leadership behavior, close performance gaps, and return to stable, or even strong performance.

Sometimes that happens. Sometimes it doesn't.

But the key distinction lies in *mindset.*

If you enter a PIP assuming the person cannot improve, then it is no longer a Performance Improvement Plan; it becomes a termination plan used primarily for documentation. While documentation is often required as part of a formal termination process, the spirit of a PIP should include the possibility of improvement.

As a leader, there should be a genuine window of opportunity in your mind that if the individual improves, that is a win for them, for the team, and for the organization.

By the time someone reaches this stage, the focus should be:

- Narrow and clear

- Anchored in specific leadership or performance competencies

- Tied to measurable actions and firm timelines

Nothing on a PIP should be a surprise. These issues should have been addressed through prior feedback and development conversations.

I often think of PIPs in terms of return on investment.
You are investing more time, attention, and coaching. There must be visible progress in return. When someone is moving in the right direction, you lean in. When they're not, the focus remains tight, and the expectations stay high.

Many steps lead to a PIP. By the time you get here, precision matters.

This Isn't Everything, But It's Enough to Get You Moving

This list isn't exhaustive. It's not meant to be. But it gives you tactical steps to help you know:

- When to step in

- What to do

- How to guide performance forward

This should give you enough to move confidently through *Develop and reach Advance* with intention and leadership clarity.

Sources

Bossidy, L., Charan, R., & Burck, C. (2002). *Execution: The discipline of getting things done.* Crown Business.

Day, D. V. (2001). Leadership development: A review in context. *Leadership Quarterly, 11*(4), 581–613.

Graen, G. B., & Uhl-Bien, M. (1995). Relationship-based approach to leadership: Development of LMX theory. *Leadership Quarterly, 6*(2), 219–247.

Kluger, A. N., & DeNisi, A. (1996). The effects of feedback interventions on performance. *Psychological Bulletin, 119*(2), 254–284.

Locke, E. A., & Latham, G. P. (2002). Building a useful theory of goal setting and task motivation. *American Psychologist, 57*(9), 705–717.

PART V

ADVANCE

SUSTAINING AND ELEVATING TALENT

Advance

Advance is all about structure, planning, and intention. To advance someone to a larger role, a higher level, or a strategic mindset, you must be intentional about assignments and development to enhance learning and encourage mastery.

Chapter Eleven

Talent Visibility, Succession, & Intentional Planning

Create Pipelines, Not Emergency Backfills

Strong organizations don't scramble when someone leaves; they're ready. That's because great leaders focus on building pipelines, not reacting to emergencies.

Creating a pipeline is an ongoing process of intentional development. It requires you and your leadership team to consistently identify not only the positions and levels to plan for but also the specific gaps each person must close to be considered "ready".

I want to explain, *"ready" doesn't mean perfect. Nobody will ever be perfect.* It means someone has demonstrated proficiency in their current role and shows the capacity to step into the next level of leadership or responsibility.

This is where knowing how to assess performance vs. potential is essential.

Performance vs. Potential

Leaders often confuse performance and potential. Here's a breakdown:

- **Performance** is how well someone is doing in their current role. It includes achieving results, demonstrating key skills, and consistently meeting or exceeding expectations.

- **Potential** is a person's capacity to grow into future roles. It reflects traits such as learning agility, leadership presence, strategic thinking, and the ability to take on a broader scope or greater complexity.

A top performer today may not automatically have the potential to lead tomorrow. Conversely, someone with high potential still requires development, intentional exposure to stretch opportunities, and a proven track record in their current position.

PERFORMANCE VS. POTENTIAL: A COMPARISON

Dimension	Performance	Potential
Focus	Present, how well the person executes today	Future: how well they could perform in larger or more complex roles
Indicators	Results delivered, goals met, KPIs achieved	Learning agility, leadership capacity, growth mindset
Time Horizon	Short-term impact	Long-term trajectory
Measurement	Objective and measurable (e.g., metrics, project outcomes)	More subjective (e.g., behaviors, cognitive ability, adaptability)
Risk of Overreliance	Can lead to promoting only strong doers, not future thinkers	Can lead to over-promoting those with potential but unproven track records
Development Focus	Strengthen or deepen current skills	Expand capacity for future complexity or leadership
Talent Implication	"Strong Performer", valuable where they are now. Continue to develop.	"High Potential", invest for future succession or broader roles

Key Insight:

Not every top performer has high potential. And not every high-potential leader is currently a top performer. It's critical to develop both lenses when assessing talent, especially during succession planning or leadership selection.

While it can be tempting, avoid promoting people based on potential alone before they have a proven track record. There may be rare moments when this is necessary, but when it happens, pause and reflect. Ask yourself:

- What did we miss in our talent routines?

- Did we fail to anticipate this role opening?

- Where do we need to strengthen succession planning?

These moments aren't just staffing gaps; they're signals to improve your system.

If you've assessed someone as having potential, the next step is to build a bridge, not leap. That means:

- Exposing them to new responsibilities that reflect the challenges of the next role.

- Giving them space to practice higher-level decision-making.

- Coaching them on the leadership gaps that need to be addressed.

When you assess someone as having potential, remember, *potential still requires development.* To set someone up for success at the next level, you must intentionally expose them to the demands of the role and actively develop the leadership gaps that come with increased scope and complexity.

At the same time, don't overlook your strong performers. *Invest in them. Don't take them for granted.* Top performers are the backbone of any team. They provide stability, deliver results, and model what "great" looks like for others.

When you clearly understand what success looks like at each level, and consistently assess what individuals need to grow in either performance or potential, you stop reacting to vacancies and start *building strong, sustainable talent pipelines.*

Talent Visibility & Mobility

When you're doing the hard work of development, you also have the responsibility to ensure talent has visibility and that their personal goals are understood.

📖 Storytime: Lesson Learned

Early in my career, I learned the importance of understanding an individual's goals the hard way. In a tough-to-staff market, I was actively developing a high-performing leader for what I thought would be the perfect stretch role. He had the talent, the results, and the potential to lead his peers. As the opportunity drew closer, I finally asked:

"Where are you open to relocating?"

His response?
"I need to stay close to where I am now due to a family situation."

And just like that, the plan fell apart.
I had never asked.

As the saying goes:
To assume makes an ASS out of U and ME.

Lesson Learned: Ask early! It seems simple, and it is. Take the time to ask the simple questions:

What are your goals?
What do you want?
What is not part of your plan?

Don't just focus on what you or the organization needs. Make it your mission to understand what your people want, early and often.

This isn't about giving away confidential information. It's about creating consistent, two-way dialogue that gives you the insights to align talent to opportunity when the time is right.

When you stay curious about your team members' goals and aspirations, you're not caught off guard; you're prepared to make the right match.

Shine a Light on Talent

Development isn't just about skill-building; it's also about exposure. Both top performers and high potentials deserve to be seen. Visibility means helping talent build a network and reputation across the organization, especially with decision-makers.

There will always be a "table" where talent is discussed; make sure your people have advocates at that table. I always say:

> *Don't fight at the table when the decision is being made; do the work beforehand.*

Give your people the opportunities, relationships, and visibility that make them undeniable before the opportunities arise. Remove all the "buts". You know what I'm talking about. That person would be great, but....

It's your job as the leader to develop people and help them remove the reasons they would not be considered for a role.

The Tools

There are several essential tools leaders can use to identify, develop, and prepare future-ready talent. Among the most powerful are Succession Planning, Individual Development Plans (IDPs), the 9-Box Grid, and Destination Plans. We've already explored IDPs in the Develop section. Let's now dive into the others and define each one clearly:

Succession Planning

Succession planning is a proactive, strategic process for identifying and developing internal talent with the potential to fill key leadership or critical roles in the future. It ensures business continuity by building a bench of capable leaders ready to step in when vacancies arise from promotions, retirements, or turnover.

Key Focus Areas:

- Identifying mission-critical roles

- Assessing readiness and gaps

- Developing internal talent over time

- Reducing risk in leadership transitions

Why It Matters:

Without a clear succession plan, organizations face significant risks to business continuity. In the absence of ready-now internal talent, companies may be forced to rely on external hires, who often take longer to ramp up and may not fully understand the organizational culture.

One important note: external candidates *can* be part of your succession strategy, but they may not be available when you need them most. That's why it's critical to build both an internal and external bench. For external candidates, stay connected and keep them "warm" and engaged so that if the opportunity arises, you're not starting the relationship from scratch.

Succession is not just about replacing leaders; it's about building a strong bench of ready-now and ready-later talent.

9-Box Grid

The 9-Box is a talent assessment tool used in succession planning to evaluate individuals along two dimensions: *performance* (how well they perform their current job) and *potential* (their capacity to take on larger, more complex roles in the future). It places talent into one of nine boxes, helping leaders prioritize development and succession strategies.

9-BOX GRID BREAKDOWN

Dimension	High Potential	Moderate Potential	Low Potential
High Performance	Box 1	Box 2	Box 3
Moderate Performance	Box 4	Box 5	Box 6
Low Performance	Box 7	Box 8	Box 9

Uses:

- Identifying high-potential leaders

- Prioritizing development investments

- Supporting talent review discussions

- Planning succession for key roles

Talent Balance and the 9-Box Grid

One of the most powerful aspects of the 9-Box is its ability to reveal your *talent distribution.* It allows you to assess whether your team is balanced or overly concentrated in a specific area.

For example, it's common to see many team members categorized in *Box 5 - moderate performance and moderate potential.* But here's the truth: you don't get to stay there forever.

If someone has remained in Box 5 for multiple quarters, it's time to reevaluate. Either their performance and potential must improve, or we need to assess whether they are truly in the right box or role.

Otherwise, they're not contributing to the team or the organization meaningfully.

The 9-Box also surfaces *development trends.* If a leader continues to present the same individual in the same box over multiple talent reviews without meaningful progress, it's a cue to intervene.

Example Talent Progression (illustrative only):

- **Q1 Talent Calibration:** Matt is placed in Box 4.

- **Q2 Talent Calibration:** Matt remains in Box 4 with little to no improvement. At this stage, the leader should share a clear development plan, identify Matt's mentor, and outline specific efforts to improve his performance.

- **Q3 Talent Calibration:** Matt is still in Box 4. It's time to reassess. Is his potential rating still valid? If his performance has not improved, we may need to shift focus from "potential" to simply helping Matt succeed in his current role.

Caution:
The 9-Box should never be used in isolation. Talent calibration conversations and contextual input from multiple leaders should support 9-box assessments.

It's a snapshot, not a conclusion, meant to spark conversations and action plans.

Key Lesson:
A great leader doesn't just track where people are; they help them move. And when movement doesn't happen, they ask the tough questions and adjust accordingly.

Destination Plans

A Destination Plan is a *forward-looking development strategy* for high-potential or emerging leaders. It clearly outlines a desired future role (the "destination"), the key experiences, competencies, and milestones required to get there, and the targeted timeframe. These plans are co-created by the leader and their manager to ensure alignment with both business needs and individual aspirations. Hint: this should go hand in hand with the IDP.

Key Components:

- The specific target role (their "destination")

- Timeline to readiness

- Developmental actions or stretch assignments

- Progress checkpoints

Why It Works:
Unlike vague development plans, destination plans tie development directly to business needs and career aspirations, keeping talent focused and managers accountable for growth milestones.

It's like a GPS for career progression, clarifying the path, pace, and preparation required to reach the next level.

In Practice: How They Work Together

- Succession Planning is the strategic process.

- The 9-Box is a diagnostic tool for evaluating the current state.

- Destination Plans are the action plan to close the gap between today and readiness for future roles.

- IDP is the development plan to help performance and potential readiness.

Together, they create a dynamic system of visibility, intentional growth, and role continuity, moving beyond "who's ready now" to "how do we get them ready?"

Bringing it Together: Talent Calibration

A Talent Calibration Discussion is a structured meeting where leaders align on performance and potential ratings for their team members to ensure consistent, fair, and unbiased talent assessments across the organization.

The goal is to validate individual evaluations, challenge assumptions, and create a shared understanding of talent readiness, gaps, and development needs.

The only way talent calibration conversations work is if the team knows each other's talents, is respectful of each other's experiences, and is willing to listen and be curious.

Who Attends:

- **Direct Managers:** Present their assessments and provide evidence of performance and potential.

- **Skip-Level Leaders:** Offer broader organizational context and insights on individuals who may work cross-functionally.

- **HR Business Partners or Talent Leaders:** Facilitate the session, ensure fairness, and help document outcomes.

Why It's Important:

- **Ensures Consistency:** Talent assessments are normalized across leaders, reducing personal bias and subjectivity.

- **Builds Shared Accountability:** Leaders collectively own the pipeline, not just their individual team.

- **Identifies Patterns and Gaps:** By looking across the organization, you spot strengths, risk areas, and where development or backfill is needed.

- **Aligns Leadership:** Calibration discussions are critical inputs into succession planning and workforce planning. This alignment is key to future support for the talent.

- **Reinforces Development Culture:** It helps signal that development is ongoing and that leaders are expected to coach, not just evaluate.

Use Leadership Competencies as the Common Language

Leadership competencies should be the shared language in any talent calibration or succession planning session.

📖 Storytime: Common Language Enforces Respect

I was once facilitating a talent calibration and succession planning session with my team. We were discussing a team member who showed clear potential but struggled to deliver consistent results. During the conversation, the manager referred to the leader as "emotional," a term that did not align with our competencies.

I paused and asked, "Which leadership competency does that fall under? I don't see it in our framework." The room went quiet. The manager paused, then reframed the feedback.

That moment was more than a correction; it was a turning point. It underscored the importance of using clear, shared language when discussing talent. It also raised a deeper question: would that same descriptor have been used for every leader in the same situation? Stereotypes and experience would suggest not.

Two key insights emerged from that experience:

- ***The leader wasn't fully prepared** to discuss talent in a way that aligned with our organizational standards. That meant they might also miss the mark when giving feedback to the team.*

- ***It revealed a gap in how we were developing our leaders** to think critically and equitably about performance and potential.*

After the session, I followed up in our 1:1s. I asked the manager to walk me through each team member and explain what they were doing to support their development.

Lesson Learned: Words matter. The language you use in talent discussions must reflect your organization's leadership values, not personal judgments or assumptions. When it doesn't, pause, challenge it, and coach through it. That's how you protect your culture and build leaders who grow people, not label them.

Now let's talk about the leader's role in providing access and opportunity to the team.

Sources

Cappelli, P. (2008). *Talent on demand: Managing talent in an age of uncertainty.* Harvard Business School Press.

Church, A. H., & Rotolo, C. T. (2013). How are top companies assessing their high-potentials and senior executives? *Consulting Psychology Journal: Practice and Research, 65*(3), 199–223.

Conger, J. A., & Fulmer, R. M. (2003). Developing your leadership pipeline. *Harvard Business Review, 81*(12), 76–84.

Dries, N., Pepermans, R., & De Kerpel, E. (2008). Exploring four generations of talent management. *Human Resource Management Review, 18*(2), 109–120.

Rothwell, W. J. (2010). *Effective succession planning: Ensuring leadership continuity and building talent from within* (4th ed.). AMACOM.

Chapter Twelve

Creating a Culture of Access & Opportunity

Mentorship is vital to the team's development. And sponsorship is just as important to the team's advancement.

Mentorship vs. Sponsorship

Mentorship is a developmental relationship in which a more experienced person (the mentor) provides guidance, support, feedback, and knowledge to a less experienced individual (the mentee) to help them grow professionally and personally. Mentorship often focuses on skill-building, navigating organizational culture, and career advice, and it can occur formally or informally. Mentors help mentees reflect, set goals, and build confidence.

Key traits of mentorship are

- Focused on development and learning

- Advice-driven and experience-sharing

- Confidential and trust-based

- Often initiated by the mentee

Sponsorship

Sponsorship is a high-stakes relationship where a senior leader (the sponsor) actively advocates for and leverages their influence to create visibility, opportunities, and advancement for a high-potential employee. Unlike mentorship, which is guidance-oriented, sponsorship is action-oriented: the sponsor puts their reputation on the line to promote the person they sponsor. They use their organizational capital to support the team member.

Key traits of sponsorship are

- Focused on advancement and visibility

- Influence-driven and opportunity-creating

- Often occurs behind closed doors

- Typically initiated by the sponsor, based on performance and potential

In my dissertation research, I found that some leaders receive both *mentorship and sponsorship*, while others receive mentorship alone. The difference matters. Without sponsorship, even high-potential leaders can stall, lacking the visibility, advocacy, and organizational support needed to advance.

As a leader, it is *your responsibility* to ensure your talent approach is balanced, intentional, and free from bias. That means actively ensuring your high-potential talent is not only developing skills but also building the right networks and receiving *real sponsorship*, not just advice.

Courageous Leadership in Talent Decisions

Bias is often invisible to those in power, even to decision-makers. Bias can show up around gender, ethnicity, background, experience, leadership style, competencies, or familiarity. And many times, it's unintentional.

That's why it's the responsibility of the leader in the room to recognize bias when it shows up, and to design processes that reduce it and call it out.

This is especially critical during talent discussions.

Creating structure, using shared leadership competencies, asking specific questions, and strengthening your emotional intelligence all help surface bias and limit its influence. Courageous leadership isn't about calling people out; it's about *calling the process up.*

Why This Matters

Yes, it's the right thing to do.
But it's also the smart thing to do.

Ensuring the *right people* advance strengthens the business, the team, and the customer experience. And the "right person" isn't the one everyone likes the most, it's the person who is most qualified, team-minded, business-savvy, and willing to make tough decisions in service of the organization's goals.

That's how you build trust.
That's how you build performance.

That's how you build a future-ready organization. That generates productivity and profit.

We've talked about creating a culture of opportunity. Now, let's discuss clear steps to get you there: awareness, action, and accountability.

Sources

Hewlett, S. A. (2013). *Forget a mentor, find a sponsor: The new way to fast-track your career.* Harvard Business Review Press.

Ibarra, H., Carter, N. M., & Silva, C. (2010). Why men still get more promotions than women. *Harvard Business Review, 88*(9), 80–85.

Kouzes, J. M., & Posner, B. Z. (2017). *The leadership challenge* (6th ed.). Wiley.

Nishii, L. H., & Mayer, D. M. (2009). Do inclusive leaders help to reduce turnover in diverse groups? *Journal of Applied Psychology, 94*(6), 1412–1426.

Ragins, B. R., & Kram, K. E. (Eds.). (2007). *The handbook of mentoring at work: Theory, research, and practice.* Sage Publications.

Chapter Thirteen

The 3A Talent Transformation Framework™

I know leaders love a model, and for good reason. A powerful model makes ideas easier to remember, easier to teach, and easier to apply across different situations.

That's exactly why I created the 3A Talent Transformation Framework™, based on my dissertation findings.

For the dissertation, I interviewed C-suite retail leaders to discuss their talent routines and, if they did, how they changed their talent culture to assess, identify, and develop top talent fairly.

The results showed that every leader who changed their talent pipeline, mix, and potential did so through awareness, action, and accountability. This now becomes a set of guiding principles designed to anchor your talent efforts in clarity, intention, and results.

3A isn't about checking boxes or following a rigid formula. It's about building a talent strategy that works, one that drives performance, supports development, and adapts to the evolving needs of your team and business. It brings structure, focus, and flexibility to how you attract, select, develop, and advance talent at every level.

Coach Quen's 3A Talent Transformation Framework

Awareness. Action. Accountability.

Awareness

First, the leaders built awareness.

They were explicit about what needed to change, why it mattered, the process, and what success would look like. This wasn't vague messaging; it was clear, intentional communication that set expectations across the organization.

Awareness means:

- Naming what is happening in your talent system

- Being honest about biases, gaps, and patterns

- Clarifying what success actually looks like

- Explaining the "why" behind the change

Leaders who shifted their talent outcomes didn't whisper about it. They made it visible. They explained what needed to happen and why it mattered to the business.

Awareness creates alignment.
Alignment reduces confusion.
Clarity reduces resistance.

Without awareness, change feels random. With awareness, it feels intentional.

Action

Second, they turned awareness into action.

These leaders embedded concrete action steps into the culture. Teams weren't just talking about talent; they were creating and executing plans to identify, grow, and advance it. Development wasn't left to chance; it was designed.

Awareness without action is performative.

The leaders who changed their talent outcomes didn't stop at conversation. They implemented concrete steps:

- Who owns development conversations?

- What does succession planning look like?

- How are high-potentials identified?

- What experiences must be earned?

- What changes in hiring processes?

Action includes:

- Clear ownership

- Defined timelines

- Specific behavioral expectations

- Documented processes

It's not "We should do better."
It's "Here's exactly what we are doing, who is responsible, and by when."

If you can't point to action, you don't have change; you have intention.

Accountability

Third, they layered in accountability.

And this is where most efforts fail. Accountability wasn't symbolic; it was structural. It showed up in performance reviews, leadership goals, and ongoing business discussions. It wasn't a poster on the wall or a talking point in meetings. It mattered.

The leaders who succeeded didn't rely on goodwill. They embedded accountability into the system:

* Talent development showed up in performance reviews.

* Succession strength impacted executive evaluations.

* Outcomes were tied to bonus, merit, and advancement.

* Leaders were asked to defend their talent decisions.

When talent outcomes affect compensation and advancement, behavior changes.

Accountability moves talent strategy from aspiration to execution.

Overall, what stood out most was this:
No matter the organization or starting point, these leaders quickly changed the culture around talent.

Not "over time".

Meaningful change happened fast.

Why the 3A Framework Works

Awareness shifts mindset.
Action shifts behavior.
Accountability shifts culture.

Together, they create sustainable change.

Not in five years.
Not as a "marathon".
But through disciplined leadership.

Now, let's dig into reflection and next steps!

Sources

Dobbin, F., & Kalev, A. (2016). Why diversity programs fail. Harvard Business Review, 94(7–8), 52–60.

Kalev, A., Dobbin, F., & Kelly, E. (2006). Best practices or best guesses? Assessing the efficacy of corporate diversity policies. American Sociological Review, 71(4), 589–617.

Kotter, J. P. (1996). Leading change. Harvard Business School Press.

Schein, E. H., & Schein, P. A. (2017). Organizational culture and leadership (5th ed.). Wiley.

Whitmore, Q. (2021). *Gender role beliefs of male senior leaders in retail and the impact on women's advancement* (Publication No. 28768295) [Doctoral dissertation, University of Southern California]. ProQuest Dissertations & Theses Global.

PART VI

REFLECT & TOOLS

Reflect

Reflection is one of the most powerful and most underutilized leadership practices.

A reflective leader:

- Learns and applies insights

- Knows themselves

- Leads with humility

- Owns mistakes

- Course-corrects with intention

As you saw in the model, *Reflect* is not a final step; it *circles the entire framework.* Reflection should happen continuously, not just at the end. After each stage of the Talent Lifecycle, and throughout the process, you should pause, assess, and adjust.

Leadership growth does not come simply from experience; it comes from reflecting on that experience and adjusting how we lead going forward.

Reflection is how learning turns into progress.

If you're struggling to attract talent, reflect.

- Where are you looking?

- What does your network actually look like?

- Are the people recruiting aligned on what "great" truly means?

If you hired the wrong person, even when you genuinely believed they were the right fit, reflect.

- Where did the process break down?

- Do your interview questions need refinement?

- Did bias, assumptions, or lack of structure creep in?

If your team isn't growing or progressing, reflect.

- What do they need more or less from you as a leader?

You get the point.

Reflection is not about blame or regret. It's about *learning faster, leading better, and evolving with intention.* Leaders who build reflection into their routines don't repeat the same mistakes; they refine their approach and strengthen their impact over time.

This is how leaders and organizations continue to grow.

Chapter Fourteen

Your Actionable Toolkit

4-Week Action Plan

Adding Structure to Your Talent Routines

Building a strong talent system doesn't require a massive overhaul. It requires intentional routines, clear expectations, and consistent follow-through. Use this four-week action plan to begin strengthening the structure around how you attract, develop, and advance talent.

4-WEEK ACTION PLAN

Week	Action	Ask/Explain/Do
Week 1: Awareness	Identify needs & evaluate current leadership routines	• Identify gaps in structure. • Are interviews & feedback consistent • Are IDPs, succession, and 9-Box in place
Week 2: Alignment	Discuss changes with your team	• Explain what and why • Get the team's input on changes • Align on key routines
Week 3: Action	Implement new routines	• Test new routines • Schedule new sessions, IDP, Talent Calibration, etc. • Increase development-focused 1:1 discussions
Week 4-8: Accountability	Review & refine the process	• What is working well? • What feels forced or unclear? • Where are we seeing improvement in talent discussions or development? • What adjustments should we make?

Week 1: Assess Your Current Talent Routines

Focus: Awareness

Start by taking a clear look at your current routines. Many leaders believe they have strong talent systems in place, but when examined closely, the processes are often informal or inconsistent.

Ask yourself:

• How structured is our interview process?

- Do we have clear expectations for onboarding and development?

- Are 1:1 meetings and feedback routines consistent?

- Do we actively discuss performance vs. potential?

- Do we have IDPs and succession conversations in place?

Identify areas where structure is missing or inconsistent.

Deliverable:

Write down three talent routines that need a stronger structure.

Examples:

- Interview process

- Development planning

- Succession discussions

- Feedback routines

Week 2: Align the Team on the Changes

Focus: Alignment

Once you've identified the gaps, bring your leadership team into the conversation.

Explain:

- What will change

- Why it matters

- When it will start

Transparency and inclusion build ownership.

Ask your team:

- Where do our talent routines break down today?

- What changes would help us develop people more effectively?

- What support do you need to make these changes successful?

This conversation ensures the process is not just top-down, but team-owned.

Deliverable:

Agree on 2–3 talent routines you will strengthen together.

Week 3: Implement the New Talent Routines

Focus: Action

Now begin putting the changes into practice.

Examples of actions:

- Test new interview questions aligned to competencies

- Standardize interview recaps

- Schedule IDP conversations

- Add regular talent discussions to leadership meetings

- Increase 1:1 development conversations

- Clarify performance versus potential discussions

The goal is not perfection. The goal is practice and consistency.

Deliverable:

Implement at least two structured talent routines immediately.

Weeks 4–8: Reflect and Adjust

Focus: Accountability

Strong leadership routines require reflection.

After several weeks of implementing your changes, ask:

- What is working well?

- What feels forced or unclear?

- Where are we seeing improvement in talent discussions or development?

- What adjustments should we make?

Reflection is where learning happens.

Use feedback from your team and early results to refine your process.

Deliverable:

Make one improvement to the new routines based on what you've learned.

Leadership Reminder

Structure does not slow down talent development; it accelerates it.

When leaders add clarity to hiring, development, and advancement routines, they create a culture of development where talent is consistently identified, supported, and elevated.

Small structural changes today create stronger leadership pipelines tomorrow.

The Tools:

Download your free tools by scanning the QR code below or clicking the link in your ebook.

https://shop.coachquen.com/products/hire-right-keep-great-people-digital-downloads

Many of the tools referenced in this book are common talent management tools readily available through a simple internet search or an AI request. I don't claim to have any special formats that make these tools more effective than what is already available. In fact, I encourage you to do a little digging and find the versions of succession plans, 9-Box grids, destination plans, and Individual Development Plan (IDP) templates that work best for you and your organization.

What matters most is not the form itself, but how intentionally you use it.

The tools that follow help you assess where you currently are in different areas of the talent lifecycle and identify where you should focus your efforts.

Coach Quen's Talent Lifecycle Self-Assessment for Leaders

This self-assessment helps you identify which sections of Coach Quen's Talent Lifecycle you should focus on to improve. Use this assessment to understand yourself better and identify areas of improvement.

Building Psychological Safety & Belonging Checklist

This checklist gives you concrete questions to identify what you are doing great in building a culture of belonging and what you need to focus on. Use this checklist when you are assessing your current environment, building culture, and teaching teams how to be part of a culture of belonging.

Rules of Engagement

This tool was highlighted in the Accountability Advantage. Team norms are where the team co-creates how they want to work together, how they show up, communicate, and hold each other accountable.

Sources

Day, D. V. (2001). Leadership development: A review in context. *Leadership Quarterly, 11*(4), 581–613.

Dewey, J. (1933). *How we think: A restatement of the relation of reflective thinking to the educative process.* D.C. Heath.

Kolb, D. A. (1984). *Experiential learning: Experience as the source of learning and development.* Prentice-Hall.

Mezirow, J. (1991). *Transformative dimensions of adult learning.* Jossey-Bass.

Schön, D. A. (1983). *The reflective practitioner: How professionals think in action.* Basic Books.

Conclusion

Culture of Development

With structure, intention, and ownership, you can transform the culture around talent in your organization or department, creating a culture of development.

With a culture of development:

- You are building a workplace where people want to stay, grow, and contribute.

- You are advancing talent progression with intention.

- You are aligning systems and actions to evolve your talent ecosystem.

- Creating high-performing organizations that are built and sustained.

Legacy of Talent

Many leaders aim to build a legacy, focusing on behavior, reputation, and personal brand. But often, they overlook the most powerful legacy of all:

Your team is your leadership legacy.

The strength, growth, and performance of the team you build is what remains long after you've moved on. Whether you're still in the role or have advanced to something greater, your team will carry forward the culture, mindset, and standards you instilled.

What you do today shapes the next generation of leaders, the ones who will carry the torch tomorrow.

Now that's a legacy worth building.

The ROI of Intentional Talent Routines

I've always viewed leadership through the lens of ROI, return on investment. Where you spend your time, what you give your attention to, and the metrics you choose to track, all matter.

You can't expect a return if you haven't made an intentional investment.

This book is your invitation, an invitation to lead with clarity, courage, and intention.

To lead with structure, focus, and determination.

To lead with legacy.

About Dr. Quendrida Whitmore

Dr. Quendrida Whitmore (Coach Quen®) is an executive coach, team architect, and organizational leadership strategist who helps high-performing organizations do what many struggle to sustain: build a culture where trust is real, expectations are clear, and accountability doesn't feel like blame, it feels like ownership.

After more than 25 years leading in complex, results-driven environments, Quendrida understands what breaks performance at scale. In roles spanning Target, Ross Stores, and WeWork, she led large, distributed teams where execution mattered daily and where culture wasn't a slogan, it was a business lever. Those experiences shaped her core belief: high-performing organizations don't happen by accident; they're built by leaders who create clarity, model accountability, and reinforce ownership at every level.

Today, Quendrida partners with executives and leadership teams to strengthen how they lead through disciplined routines, aligned expectations, and trust-building behaviors that hold under pressure. Her approach blends enterprise operator experience with doctoral-level insight in organizational change, helping leaders translate leadership theory into actions teams can actually follow. Her vision is bold and simple: "rid the world of bad bosses™," upskilling them with leaders who know how to develop people and deliver results.

She is the author of The Accountability Advantage: 5 Proven Steps to Build a Culture of Trust, Ownership, and Results, a practical framework designed to help leaders end micromanagement, stop over-functioning, and create a culture where people rise and own outcomes even when the leader isn't in the room.

Quendrida has also contributed to leadership conversations in the hospitality space through Boston University's ecosystem, including serving as Executive-in-Residence at the School of Hospitality Administration. Whether coaching a C-suite leader, facilitating a leadership team reset, or keynoting on accountability and culture, she equips leaders to build teams that execute with trust, clarity, and momentum.

About Quendrida Whitmore Coaching & Consulting

Coach Quen is dedicated to empowering individuals and organizations to achieve their fullest potential through transformative coaching and leadership development programs.

Our mission is to foster an environment of growth and innovation, where diverse talents are nurtured and turned into dynamic leadership capabilities, ensuring that every client cannot only meet but exceed their personal and professional goals. We strive to create a more inclusive and equitable world, one leader at a time.

Our Services:

- **Leadership Workshops:** Group and organizational training to help transform teams.

- **Team Building & Org Agility:** Leverage individual strengths, build trust, and set goals for success.

- **Executive Coaching:** One-on-one coaching to help you realize your life's purpose.

- **Career Coaching:** Guidance, consulting & mentoring on your current career or a new one.

- **Speaker & Panelist:** Need a dynamic and experienced speaker? Book Coach Quen®!

Core Values

- **Self-awareness:** Encouraging a deep understanding of one's strengths, weaknesses, emotions, and motivations. This awareness enables individuals to lead with authenticity, make informed decisions, and foster meaningful relationships in personal and professional settings.

- **Empowerment:** Facilitating personal and professional growth to enable individuals and organizations to reach their fullest potential.

- **Innovation:** Promoting creative solutions and continuous improvement in leadership practices.

- **Diversity and Inclusion:** Building an inclusive environment where diverse talents are nurtured into dynamic leadership capabilities.

- **Commitment and Involvement:** Creating a sense of commitment and involvement through purpose-driven actions and decisions. Intentional actions.

Visit us at CoachQuen.com to learn more!